GOD in
my DAY

GOD in my DAY

Glenn H. Asquith

ABINGDON PRESS

NASHVILLE & NEW YORK

God in My Day

Copyright © 1967 by Abingdon Press

Library of Congress Catalog Card Number 67-22170

SET UP, PRINTED, AND BOUND BY THE
PARTHENON PRESS, AT NASHVILLE,
TENNESSEE, UNITED STATES OF AMERICA

Dedicated to
Helen, wife beloved,
with whom I have started
and ended many days

Preface

Peter reminded us that with God a thousand years are as one day, and one day as a thousand years. There is great similarity between one day in the life of a person and his entire life-span. Awakening in the morning is a figure of birth; sleep at night is much like death. And, in between awakening and sleep, there are events which are small parts of happenings across the years. This book has the dual purpose of exhibiting the fascination and worth of one day while leading the reader through the vicissitudes of his whole existence.

It is recognized that some things are experienced occasionally rather than regularly, and these rarer occurrences are woven into the fabric of the text in a way, it is hoped, to avoid confusion.

I have used the first person in order that each reader may talk to himself and examine his own hopes and longings and needs rather than take the stand-off attitude of one who passes judgment on what some other person is thinking.

Perhaps to some extent we all have lost or pushed aside the great truth that life is the gift of God and is limitless in possibilities day by day. This book is intended as a help toward recovering this exciting element of being.

Glenn H. Asquith

Contents

I

MORNING—and EVENING

II
DAWN—until DUSK

CONTENTS

I
MORNING...
and EVENING

Things and experiences of daily living . . .
the routine and expected . . .
all that could be called monotonous
but which can be exciting

AWAKENING

"It is of the Lord's mercies that we are not consumed, because his compassions fail not. *They are new every morning:* great is thy faithfulness." (Lamentations 3:22-23)

I was born this morning!

Of course this is not the day noted on my birth certificate, but, even so, I was born this morning. This is a birthday for me. And I was born yesterday, and the day before, and the day before that. As a matter of fact, I have had 365 or 366 births every year of my life.

Every morning at my awakening I come as a new person into a new world. However, I am conditioned by my past experience, which is my privilege and warning. On my first birthday as a baby, I had the same conditioning through my heritage and potentialities for good or ill. The ages were waiting to unfold in me then as now. A birth is always an exciting thing filled to the brim with all kinds of possibilities.

I pause for the first moment of today's birth. Soon I shall stir to take my place in this little period of history and of God's purpose. I am conscious, once more, of God's great and good gift of awareness. The earth on which I live reaches out to touch me with small sounds and odors and sights. From the out-of-doors the world seeps in through closed windows and shutters. Small creakings in the otherwise stillness of the house remind me that nothing man-made is proof against the eternal forces exerted against our puny walls to assure me that God *is*.

And I sense this same gentle pressure in my inner being. I am not complete of myself. God insistently and healingly pushes against my regrets and despair, and suffuses my soul with his hope and comfort.

Every morning at my birth to another day, all this evidence of God comes to me as I awaken. I lie quiet for a little time to comtemplate this new life-in-a-day and to thank God that I am to be given another chance for better and more obedient service in a needy place. There is no limit set to the surprises that may cross my path or come into my dwelling. Of one thing I may be sure—

this will be a day unlike any other day past or future, and it is mine!

Prayer of a New Day: My Father, I feel the quivering of events about to take place, and I await with hope and confidence what is to come to me. No gift of thine can be other than good for me. Make me worthy of being here at this hour. *Amen.*

SOMEBODY IN THE HOUSE

Jesus said, "I am with you alway." (Matthew 28:20)

A small boy who was about to be tucked in bed for the night asked, "But who will be with me when I am by myself?"

This question comes to me at every morning awakening. Am I alone?

17

The rattle of pans in the kitchen, the sound of water turned on in the bathroom, a footstep heard in an adjoining room, other stirrings which are sure proof that companionship is near, comfort me—somebody is in the house.

This happy knowledge is mine only when I am fortunate enough to be living with family or friends, or as one of several or many in a residence for single people.

But what about the time or times when I am away from loved ones or associates of the years, when I am occupying a hotel room, an apartment or other dwelling where I am the only one there? How can I stand it if there is nobody in the house? The older I get, the more likely this is to be my lot, as I realize full well. "Who will be with me when I am by myself?"

And I answer myself by faith. I am not alone. I shall never be alone. There will be Somebody in the house always. The Lord is ever near me as he has promised.

Of course I cannot expect God to rattle a pan in the kitchen, turn on a faucet somewhere, cause the boards to creak with his walking; but I can know that he is present. "Closer is He than breathing, and nearer than hands or feet."

From past experience I know that this assurance of God's nearness is not superstition or wishful thinking. When I have yielded myself to the mystery of being God's child, I have known him to make himself known in my sorrows and joys, in my losses and my triumphs. I cannot explain this to anyone, but I know it to be true.

As I lie quietly in my bed knowing that I have been born to a new day, I wait until I become aware of that Somebody in the house. Silently or audibly I speak to him of my concerns for this new day; I ask for directions and guidance; I express thanksgiving for the night that is past; I enjoy God. And answers come. From the Person who never deserts me, I gain strength as flowers flourish in the light of the sun.

Together, that Somebody in the house and I prepare me for whatever is to befall.

Thanksgiving for Companionship: Father of all lonely children, I thank thee for the loved ones and friends who have kept me from solitude through the years; but, most of all, I thank thee that thou art the one who will never leave me or forsake me. *Amen.*

ARISING

"Arise . . . and be doing, and the Lord be with thee." (I Chronicles 22:16)

Awakening and prayer are good, but I realize that I have awakened for the purpose of arising. In the accounts of Jesus' miracles of raising the dead to life or of healing the lame or paralytic, his word was always—Arise! There is something to be done in the world for humanity and for God.

In a sense my arising is a symbol of my eventual resurrection from the dead, just as sleep is a symbol of what I call death. On this new morning of my life I am called back from immobility to motion. Creation is in movement. The heavenly bodies are whirling along to keep their appointed positions from hour to hour; the earth is turning on its axis and revolving around the sun; in the earth seeds are working; the birds and other creatures are busily engaged in their determined pursuits. I too must arise.

Even though I may be confined to bed in hospital or home, be in a wheelchair, or be almost motionless from some illness or accident, nevertheless the arising is my change from unawareness to sharp awareness that I am part of the thinking and acting world in which God has placed me. If I do not move too much, my mind and eyes will move to declare boldly that I have my place in what is going on. And when I am in possession of my health and strength, how wonderful to get out of bed and stretch and walk!

A writer of an early day has spoken of man as being "wonderfully made." How true that is I sense now as I get up and find that I have powers to go here and go there, to control my legs and arms, to arrange *things to* my own desire.

But then I ask, what difference does my arising make in the plan of God for this day? Would I have been missed if I had not got up to accept my share in the happenings of this day? And I know the answer. Unless I appear where I am expected, the telephone will ring or there will be a rap on the door, "What's the matter? Aren't you awake yet?" Someone or some task would miss me—*me!*

There are billions of people in the world, but not one who can do the things, say the word, or think the thought that God has purposed through me. No matter how insignificant I think myself to be, no matter how restricted my movements may be just now, somewhere, either in this bedroom or outside, there is an emptiness in some heart or mind or soul, there is some piece of craftmanship simple or complex, there is a gap in some team or circle waiting for me to come. I will arise and be doing!

A Plea for Energy: O Lord of life and brimful life, if this is a day when I shall be confined to a small area, give me the will to use what energy is mine to good effect; if this is a day when I am able to go and come at will, may I covenant with thee to be an able servant. *Amen.*

GREETING THE FAMILIAR

"Remove not the ancient landmark." (Proverbs 22:28)

A man who traveled extensively in his occupation told a friend that when he awakened in the morning he needed to spend a few moments to decide in what hotel and in what city he was. He would look at the furniture in the room, the pictures on the walls, and the view from his window to spot something familiar.

When I awaken in the morning I have this problem to some extent. My sleep has taken me by dream and meditation into a strange country, and I come back slowly to my own place. In the room are possessions that speak to me of the time they were acquired. My clothing is in the closet or drawers to remind me of my size and circumstance. Perhaps I shall see some evidences of hobbies; there are books that I have not finished, and my place is marked.

The familiar things that have not moved and have not changed since I fell asleep are precious in their ability to tell me who I am, where I am, what sort of person I am, what my age is, and what are my chief interests.

Beyond the windowpane are buildings, trees, fences, flowers, roads. Quickly I become re-oriented and I know the name of my city and my street. My height from the yard or pavement indicates whether or not I am above the first story of my dwelling. The state of the vegetation and leaves on the trees tells me the season of the year; the position of the sun alerts me to the time of day—have I overslept or am I early?

Surely, sleep is a symbol of death as I have thought many times, and awakening is like the resurrection. When I awake in the other and better world, will there be familiar things to make me feel that I know where I am; shall I feel that I belong? Do any of our ancient landmarks carry over from this life?

I have confidence that I shall not be over-whelmed by unfamiliarity. This world seems to me a showcase of the Creator, and when I enter the store I shall expect to find things such as I have seen in the window. The beauties of this earth cannot be temporary; the persons we have loved are not gone beyond recall; the dreams of my inner being cannot be without fulfilment. If I have needed landmarks for location here, may I not expect to find similar guides when I awaken in the presence of my God?

Perhaps I need to be careful how I select my surroundings and my possessions. If I have gathered to me things of worth, if I have chosen to live where my fellowman has work, sorrow, and joy to share, if the marvels of nature have not left me unresponsive, then I shall expect my final rousing to be in the midst of the best I have known.

A Prayer for Certitude: O Creator of all that is good and true, just and lovely, answer my question as to whether or not I shall be utterly confused by the unexpected in the life to come. May I have faith that this world and my neighbors have in them something eternal which I shall see again with joy when I awaken in a bright and glad morning. *Amen.*

WEATHER

"He answered and said unto them, When it is evening, ye say, It will be fair weather: for the sky is red. And in the morning, It will be foul weather to-day, for the sky is red and lowering. O ye hypocrites, ye can discern the face of the sky; but can ye not discern the signs of the times?" (Matthew 16:2-3)

I look through my window this morning to see what the weather is like. Throughout my life I have learned that there is one dependable thing in this world—the weather. I can be sure that the elements will present an ever-changing pageant, fresh each morning.

Sometimes it is snow that I see. The falling flakes bring down the dirt from the air until cleanliness and whiteness revive what purity remains in my world-exposed soul.

Or it may be that rain is slanting down, pouring from an upended flask of heaven or gently wandering to earth. Rain will slake the thirst of earth and growing things and will fill the reservoirs of great cities to keep men alive.

The day may be cloudy so that there is a subdued atmosphere about the activities of my brothers and sisters in the world. People seem quieter than usual, and automobile horns sound a bit apologetic. There is expectancy in the air because clouds are temporary—rain, snow, or clearing must follow for clouds cannot last.

This particular morning is a day when the weather is clear and bright. The sun touches all things with a majestic impartiality. The cracked and chipped and marred things are shown in their honest condition. To the more perfect surfaces, new luster is given. Shadows are cast mercifully here and there, until some humble faces or building stones are wrapped in beauty.

I feel that the weather today is teaching me much. Every variety of weather is essential to the health and wealth of mankind. Even the bitterest wind that brings sleet and ice is doing its part in the total balancing of nature.

By all this I learn that each phase of the weather and life is transient. Harsh or dreary weather will change inevitably for the better—and so will my life.

Two facts that grow out of these observations

comfort me this day. There are purpose and change in every experience. If there is a cloudy day in my inner being, I am due for something different. If this is a cheerful, bright period, I know that I will enjoy it while it lasts but accept the fact that unchanging sunshine would make a desert of the world and life.

I recall now that the Lord marked our interest in the weather and our ability to predict it by the signs in the skies. And he chided us for being able to do this while not being equally wise in reading the signs of God's dealings with men.

Vicissitudes: My Father, I watch the changes in temperature and wind and sky, but I miss often the changes of my moods and motives that could predict my happiness or misery. Make me perceptive of the signs from thee in my own life. *Amen.*

ABLUTIONS

"Wash me, and I shall be whiter than snow."
(Psalm 51:7)

Awakening brings duties, one of the first of which is to make myself clean. A Christian leader of an earlier century spoke of cleanliness as being next to godliness. Dirt is symbolic of evil, and washing always has something about it that is akin to a ritual of purification.

My body will not stay clean. Here I have been sleeping in a bed and in a room that are well laundered and well kept, but there has been some accumulation through the hours that makes me feel that I cannot move among my family, friends, or fellow workers without washing myself.

I know that there is more than dirt to be removed, for the very fact of using water and soap on hands and face and body brings a sense of well-being. When Jesus washed the feet of the disciples, one of them was so exuberant that he wanted his hands and face—everything—washed, but Jesus said that by washing the feet all was clean.

Of course, I know what is happening to me. When I wash I think of the removal of sin. Often I have read in the Bible of the rites of purification and how water represents the pouring of forgiveness over a soiled soul. The psalmist begged the Lord to wash him that he might be clean; he was not thinking of the clinging dust of the road or of the sand that the desert wind had blown upon him; he was thinking of his iniquities.

And so I go where the water is available in my house, from faucet, bowl, or well. I plunge myself into the liquid and find that a healthy glow shows on my skin and that an inner glow can be felt. Although I may not be handsome in appearance, I have made myself clean out of respect for those with whom I shall associate today and out of my reverence for God. With all my faults I have done what I could.

And as many mornings as I am permitted to awaken in this world, I shall use what strength I have to perform my morning ablutions. This simple act will be my admission to all men and to the Lord that I have need of forgiveness, and that I am crying out for the eternal and permanent washing away of all my sins, so that I shall be as white as snow.

A Prayer Thought: O Thou who movest in the white light where no darkness is, help me to know as I go through the routine bathing of the morning that there is a grace to cleanse me from all sin and make me worthy to appear in thy sight. *Amen.*

MEDITATION

"His delight is in the law of the Lord; and in his law doth he meditate day and night." (Psalm 1:2)

Greater, but frequently unrecognized, is my hunger for the bread of life than for the bread of the pantry; greater is my thirst for the water of life than for the orange juice in the refrigerator.

Therefore, before I break my fast I sit or stand quietly and consider the law of the Lord.

By the mysterious law of the Lord I live on a round world, but I can look in any direction without observing the earth's curve. I live on a revolving and rotating planet, but I sense no uneasiness of motion or upside-downness.

At times I plant a seed in the garden or in a window box and have no doubt that, by the law of the Lord, a green shoot will appear in due time. By this I know that my food and the food of all mankind is assured year after year, century after century. The raging of men of ill will, the rise and fall of governments, millions of deaths and births cannot alter the law of growth.

As the sun begins to shine upon me this day, or as I move under cloudy skies, I can have no misgivings that all the heavenly bodies are in their places moving at a predestined speed in directions assigned by the law of the Lord.

All of this comforts me. The world I am about to explore for another day is well ordered and well cared for. I may concentrate on other concerns knowing that I have a base of operations that is dependable and predictable.

This assurance, however, is not sufficient of itself to send me forth in triumph. I meditate longer on the law of the Lord written in my heart.

The law tells me that faith is always rewarded, that the struggle for goodness brings overflowing returns, that no worthy thought or motive or deed will blow back empty on the wind.

And so I am ready for the day. By obeying and living within the law of the Lord I shall not be insignificant, and evening will not find me with unfilled hands.

In Awe and Gratitude: O Lord, thy law is too wonderful for my understanding. My thanks go out that I live in a world of purpose and that my life is not an aimless happenstance. *Amen.*

MORNING MEAL

"The meek shall eat and be satisfied." (Psalm 22:26)

I find myself in danger!

I am hungry, and my life depends upon the satisfying of that physical need of the body.

Of course I am not desperately hungry—just comfortably hungry. The thought of eggs and bacon, of waffles or griddle cakes, of toast and jelly, a cinnamon bun, milk, cereal brings pleasant anticipation.

But hunger is an affliction. It is a sign of mortality. I am moved from my uplifting morning meditation into my place as a human among humans.

It is good that I know this. Even though I am about to enjoy my breakfast before my craving becomes painful, recurring hunger reminds me that I have this affliction in common with all men. In sorrow I recall that starvation is constant in many areas of the world.

I thank God for hunger because it links me in sympathy with my brothers and sisters. I realize that I am not privileged to be immune above others, and that no amount of money, family love, or favorable circumstances can keep me from the necessity of taking regular nourishment. An emaciated child in India is experiencing what I am now experiencing—except that his hunger is far more acute. Our affliction is in common.

My joy as I sit down to the deliciousness of a morning meal is not changed to utter sorrow, but I am sobered as I think of the many who will eat sparingly, if at all, at this hour. This part of my day becomes a holy event, a sacrament.

The solid good taste of bread and the flavor of an orange become infinitely more than appetite teasers; they stand for the bond between my need and God's provision. Eating and drinking are rituals observed by me in my room while my brothers are doing the same in thousands of places around the world.

But am I partaking of this breakfast just to keep alive? Just to assuage the hunger pangs? Is this what God intended?

I must feel that there is a deeper meaning to my daily yielding to a physical need. Strengthened by the food, I know that the strength is required of me to be expended in a way that will not shame the labors of the farmers and others who have given much of their lives to feed me.

Life spent calls for life to be spent. There is work waiting to be done. By breakfasting I have pledged myself to continue the unbroken line of workmen stretching back to God the Creator, and I look forward to the time when I shall eat only of the bread of life.

For Food in the Morning: My Father, I thank thee for the satisfying of my early hunger. I thank thee for all who have gone out into the fields and barns and orchards to make it possible for me to live in this world another day. *Amen.*

FORENOON WORK

"But Jesus answered them, My Father worketh hitherto, and I work." (John 5:17)

I have energy!

The thrill of awakening to this day, the spiritual and mental fortification by meditation and prayer, the physical renewal from food at breakfast have charged me as a battery is charged.

What shall I do with the potential power within me?

My condition seems to me much like that of a propeller driven airplane waiting at the end of a runway at a great airport; all the engines are roaring, the propellers are whirling so fast that the blades cannot be seen, and the whole ship is trembling violently, pulling against the brakes until the pilot releases the restraints and frees it to fly.

Or I think of a steam locomotive with its boiler filled with steam ready for channeling to the pistons to turn the great wheels and start on a long trip to haul useful things to distant cities.

When will the throttle be opened and the power unleashed?

The energy within me of one kind or another may be set to work this morning or I may let it go to waste. Occasionally an airplane is ordered back to the hangar with its flight canceled; occasionally a locomotive is unhooked from its train and returned to the shop. How sad to know that that flight or run will never be made! And worst of all, the energy which was for a particular purpose is forever wasted.

I must not waste *my* energy—I must find a forenoon's work and get about my Father's business. Unless, of course, this is one day that the Lord sees fit to cancel the effort temporarily.

To what then may I set my hand and mind? Simple tasks perhaps, possibly complex jobs— labor in the home, labor beyond my dwelling in school, factory, office, store, or elsewhere. My main consideration will be to get something done that is essential to God's purpose in the world and in the lives of my fellowmen.

I know that I shall not work alone; possibly I shall work with others, but certainly I shall work with God by my side. This morning I have read that the Creator does not consider his six days of labor enough—he *still* works. And our Lord is working, too. What company!

As I do what has been given me to do I have a warm feeling of making an eternal contribution in and to the great plan of life which was set in motion so long ago and which is to come to perfection in God's good time. I am doing something this morning that no one else has been appointed to do. My morning's work is like the work of my youth and early maturity—a good piece of labor while my strength is equal to the task.

I feel that I am significant because of my work and that I am needed and necessary.

For Work: My Father, and the Father of all who come to thee, help me to understand why I have the task which is mine. Give me a sense of its meaning. May I be assured that my energy has been expended fruitfully. *Amen.*

REST PERIOD

"Come to me, all ye that labor and are heavy laden, and I will give you rest." (Matthew 11:28)

As I continue working I find, to my chagrin, that the task gradually drains away my strength. This, of course, is to be expected and is a wholesome circumstance. When Jesus was touched by a woman in need of healing he knew that something had gone out from him. By this example I know that unless I am giving of my very self, I have accomplished nothing of value.

Even so, I stop and consider. There is so much to do in the world, so much thought and concern and effort are needed, and there are so few to do all that cries out to be done. Is it wise to ignore my fatigue and push on? There are times when this must be done, but ordinarily more is achieved in the long run if I stop, as I do now, to be restored to vigor. Wisdom, given of God, dictates a brief retreat before a new and more vigorous advance.

Earlier in my day, when my energy was surging with impatience to be harnessed to a job, I thought of myself as a fully charged battery. Now I think of a period of inactivity as a time for recharging that battery. There are flashlights from which the exhausted battery may be removed and plugged into a wall outlet. After a period of time that same battery may be replaced in the flashlight, and it will give a strong illumination for poking around in dark places. As my body relaxes I sense that I am in connection with the great Source of power, and that there is a quiet renewal like an incoming tide restoring strength to jaded nerves, muscles, and mind.

In fact, I have been invited to stop for awhile. When I find myself weary and heavy laden I know where to find my rest. Not in stimulants of one sort or another, not in physical rituals, not in worldly recreation, but in companionship with the Eternal do I come to newness of life.

I remember an advertisement of an automobile manufacturer: "When your car is in need of repairs or service, bring it back to the man who sold it to you—he knows your car and he has the parts that fit." Good advice! And should I not go, when I need service or repairs, back to my Creator who knows me and can replace my energy from

41

the same bountiful supply that gave me first the strength which I have expended this morning?

A strange lesson is taught me during my short rest period. I find it was not my arms, my legs, my back that required the renewal, but my soul. Doctors have learned this too. They call it the "mental outlook on life" that makes the difference between vigor and listlessness. With God, I think I must call my weary part the spirit. He touches my fountainhead and all is changed. As with Peter, whose feet the Lord washed and who wanted his hands and head washed also, but was told that if the feet were clean all is clean, so I find that one point of contact with Power is all that I need.

Every morning in mid-task I have found my way back to fresh exhilaration. This foretells to me the plan of the Heavenly Father for pauses in my larger lifework. Whenever rest is needed, rest is provided, together with a new joy to take back to the work.

Thinking of Life: O thou All-Wise and All-Loving, I thank thee for the rhythm of life—for the pattern of labor and rest, labor and rest. Both are blessings to me because given by thee. *Amen.*

MAIL

"As cold waters to a thirsty soul, so is good news from a far country." (Proverbs 25:25)

I suppose that a rest period is something like a Mount of Transfiguration insofar as there is the temptation to make rest the main business of life instead of a necessity and a reward for energy well expended. After a rest period I reluctantly realize that the work of the world does not get done automatically. But sometimes there is a pleasant interruption that justifies me in stopping a moment longer—the mail has come!

Who has something to say to me today, I wonder. And what has he to say? With eagerness I receive the little packet of envelopes, papers, and magazines from the carrier.

I wonder if others are as childish as I am as I turn the letters over and over trying to guess what is inside. I could open them quickly and satisfy my curiosity, but then the mystery would be gone! This crisp white envelope with no return address may be telling me that I have fallen heir to great riches, but if I open it immediately I will know that someone is going to urge me to buy a book or a gadget that will change the course of my life (so the advertisement always says).

Knowing that some useful task awaits me, I stifle my desire to dream and get at the business of reading my mail.

I find some of my dreams more than fulfilled. Someone I love or admire has sent me news from a far country—there is health and happiness in some distant home where my heart likes to wander. In my mail I find friendship, the knowledge of affairs that need my small assistance, links to the wide world beyond my doors.

There is something about my mail that is completely personal. There is a law that forbids anyone else to open a letter that bears my name. And my correspondents have spent money for postage in order to say something to *me*. I know that my name is listed in certain places and that I am not completely left out of all the action of life.

As I put away items brought by the postman, I remember that I get mail from God. There is news from a far country hidden in the words of the Bible; there is news that comes to me after prayer; there is news delivered to me by God's servants in many ways as I live out my days. Throughout my years I continue to learn of the larger life. My thirsty soul is satisfied.

As I Think of News: My Father, I feel included in all eternity when I sense that I am receiving messages to keep me aware of what is happening in thy kingdom. May I keep my sense of anticipation whenever a letter is to be opened or a verse of scripture is to be pondered. *Amen.*

TASK CONTINUED

"Commit thy works unto the Lord, and thy thoughts shall be established." (Proverbs 16:3)

When an airplane makes a stop between its origin and its final destination, passengers who get out to stretch their legs are told to place an "Occupied" card on their seats. This means that they will return to go farther on the flight. Whenever I leave a task of one kind or another, I leave some indication that I intend to come back to finish what I have started. The job is "occupied," and I do not intend to desert it half done.

Frequently I find that picking up the thread of what I have been doing is harder than beginning so eagerly in the morning. It is something like the first and second coats of paint. The first coat shows what I have done, but the second coat is not so exciting. Nevertheless, work must be done, and I get busy and find that I can pick up the tempo and that I can find joy in the use of whatever skill it is that God has given me to employ. I like to think that I am keeping the rust off, and that I am keeping supple even the smallest creative gift that is mine.

I find that I am helped to go on with the project in hand by committing all the work to my Lord. I may make plans and have great purposes, but my plans are not established by my own efforts. Sometimes I think that my plans for the tremendous things I would like to accomplish are like the film I take out of my camera. Even by holding a processed film up to the light, it is difficult to see much; the whites appear black and the blacks white. But when the film is placed next to photographic paper and exposed to light, the blacks and whites are in the proper order, and the picture is seen. My plans are somewhat in reverse until I commit them to God, and he makes them permanent and meaningful by his great light.

As I think of these things, the work prospers in my hands. I am grateful for the new strength that enabled me to come back and get on with the job.

In a way, my resumption of the work is a symbol of how I have resumed my task from day to day and year to year. There is no real retirement for God's child. The main occupation may end at age sixty-five, but there is always something else worthy of effort, if it is no more than contriving thoughts and ideas to pass on to others whose physical capacity is greater, or writing encouraging notes to younger people in the thick of life's battle.

Plea for Patience: Lord, may I have the patience to strive toward completion and quality as I go back to an unfinished task and gather up the pieces and put them together again. *Amen.*

MIDDAY MEAL

"Give us this day our daily bread." (Matthew 6:11)

Some things I can forget, but other things keep pushing themselves into my consciousness for attention. My bodily needs keep demanding that I remember them. Just now my body is reminding me that it can be used to perform some task for a certain period, but after that short time hunger, the old affliction of the race, strikes.

When I pause at noon there is a sense of being at the halfway house of the day—akin to the fortieth year of life. The day or the man is at full strength.

So I pause and select foods suitable for the needs of the coming afternoon.

As I eat I think of the prayer, "Give us this day our daily bread." How helpless we are after all!

How much better are we than a baby who awakes and cries for his bottle? The infant has no way of being satisfied unless his mother or another person brings him nourishment.

Of course I can trust the men who run the tractors to plow and harvest, I can admire the shrewd owners of fruit trees and vineyards, but I must admit that all this labor is in vain unless God gives us our food by sending rain and fruitful seasons, sunshine and the unfailing law of germination, seed time and harvest.

Before I eat I pause to thank God for giving to me and all my brothers and sisters the daily bread.

Too, I remember that when there was a great famine in the ancient lands God gave bread through raising up Joseph and giving him wisdom to conserve food in time of plenty.

Also there come back to mind other days of my life. There were times when I had so much joy and strength and hope that I could not use all my vitality and happiness. And there were other periods of weakness, sorrow, and despair when I had to draw new light from the warehouse in which the surplus of my faith had been stored. In one way or another, God always gives me my daily bread.

And so I eat while the sun stands high in the heavens; even though the skies be cloudy I know the sun is above to give light and heat.

The meal at noon is after work and before work and has an element of the first Passover, which was eaten without leisurely pausing to savor fully the flavor of the food. There was a journey to take. The rest of the day has yet to be traveled.

At Midday: For the blessings of the forenoon, and the prospect of the afternoon, and for the unfailing means of bread, Father, I am humbly thankful. *Amen.*

SIESTA

"I will both lay me down in peace, and sleep: for thou, Lord, only makest me dwell in safety." (Psalm 4:8)

Following my noonday meal I am reminded of a happy little Spanish word, "siesta," which, I am told, means "a short midday rest." How wise a custom siesta suggests!

If I have time I follow the Spanish habit and relax for a few moments. I know that it is wise to relieve the tension of activity and permit my body to go back to the Eden of creation when so little was expected of it. The knots of nerves are untwisted, and there is physical peace.

Perhaps I fall into the state between sleep and waking when dreams are half real and half unreal.

It is the time when an older person goes back to his childhood, and all cares disappear for a while; or when a younger person has visions of wonderful things to come in life.

Is it any wonder that a nap is so valued by all but children? There is something about a brief daytime sleep that is far more satisfying than the routine rest of the night. There is not enough fatigue to deaden the keen perceptions of the senses, and none of the disturbing dreams brought on by the clearing of the mind from the images impressed by its compassionate journey through the world of men for a whole day. At night the sufferings and the joys about which we hear and read or actually share become in a way our own, and must be lived vicariously before morning.

But a siesta! What a blessing from God! Sleep—peace—safety! The magic of this I often experience in hard times as well as in good. A nap is like a shaft of sunlight on a cloudy day; short, but a promise of full brightness to come before long.

As I drowse I am in the world but somehow not of it. I move in happy places among joyful people. Colors are vivid. I am at ease and quietly amused.

Could this be a little intimation of the world to

come? Everything seems so much better than I could imagine all by myself. Good thoughts and visions come unbidden. It is the kind of pleasure a child has when grown-ups accuse him of day-dreaming.

And so I enjoy my siesta.

For Peace: My Father, may the peace that comes to me so often when I stop at midday be more often mine as I yield my stubborn resistance to the quietness of the flow of life in thee. *Amen.*

AFTERNOON LABOR

"Let the favor of the Lord our God be upon us: and establish thou the work of our hands upon us; yea, the work of our hands establish thou it." (Psalm 90:17)

I find that in my day nothing is without purpose or obligation. Eating is a pleasure, but it is more than that; it is a preparation for expending strength in useful toil. And my nap is a marvelously soothing experience, but it too is given to me for a reason. I am thereby girded up in spirit for the work of the afternoon.

Afternoon work is done in the latter half of one day, but it reminds me of the work of a person beyond the age of fifty. The experimentation of the early morning and the resolution of the job in late morning give way to the positive task of putting the finishing touches on what has been started.

Returning to the scene of my effort, I stop for a moment to assess the progress of the thing in hand and lay plans for completing it within the time allotted to me before nightfall. What has been done? What is to be done?

Again I look at my contribution to life today: work among others in the accepted pursuits of the world, a solitary task of experiment or writing, something which I must do from my one room or even from my bed. Whatever it is, small or large, God has given it to me, and it is important even if it consists only of some phone calls or letters to write or helpful conversation with the lonely.

Afternoon work, because it is a finishing, reminds me of the psalmist's plea to have his work established. He did not want to feel that what he had invested his days in would vanish and be of no account after he left it. Nor do I. In many ways my work is the measure of my life. Has it been worth all that I have put into it?

So I, rather solemnly, attack the half-done job. My very best will be given in these later hours.

And I wonder how this work will be linked to the lives of others and how it will make a part of eternity. Is not this the establishing of the work?

If the favor of the Lord is upon me this afternoon I shall have the perseverance to do what I see before me, even if it is only a brave recovery from illness, or taking the first hard steps of a long recuperation.

The lengthening hours of late afternoon find me conscious of the nearness of God.

For the Permanence of Work Done: O Lord, may what I have done in my day be changed and perfected and kept, somehow, for mankind and me as part of thy purpose. *Amen.*

GOING HOME

"Then the disciples went away again unto their home." (John 20:10)

I find my task completed for the day—what now?

Why of course, I shall go home.

There is nothing so wonderful to me in the language of men as the word "home." At the end of a day or a period of life, home has a special fascination. I recall playing games as a child where there was chasing and hiding, all with an end to getting to a rock or tree which we had named "home." Could I get "home" without being caught and eliminated from the game? What a great joy and exultation to put my hand on the sanctuary of the rock or tree and cry out, "I am home free!" This old feeling of having escaped my adversaries in the day's play impels me now as I lay aside the completed piece of work. I shall go home free.

If anyone should stop me and inquire, "Where is your home?" I would reply, "Why, it is where I live." This expression we use is descriptive of the place or condition that we have made for ourselves as a haven from the turmoil, intrusions, demands, and darkness of the outer world. In that place, whether it be one room (perhaps shared with another) or a great house, are the gathered symbols of life so far. Mementos, perhaps trophies, treasured letters, a favorite chair are there, and, best of all if we are so fortunate, a loved one is waiting to share what the day has brought. Home is where I really live.

A poet has spoken of "God, who is our home." The figure of speech is so well chosen! Whatever else God is to me, he is like that place I call my home. He receives me, no matter how unworthy, after the day's work is done. In him I really live.

I think of the verse I have for today, and I picture the disciples going back to their homes thinking that all was lost and that their Lord was no more. Even in the depth of this indescribable sorrow, they thought instinctively of going home. It is so with me and others; in joy or calamity we must get home.

And so it will be, I am sure, when my life's final day is ended that I shall want to go home to be with my loving Heavenly Father.

For Home: How wonderful are thy gifts, O God, and so comforting that gift of the home feeling, and my instinct to make a place where I can really live. Keep me from sin and make me more worthy of the place of many mansions. *Amen.*

COMFORTABLE CLOTHES

"They shall put off their garments wherein they ministered, and lay them in the holy chambers, and they shall put on other garments." (Ezekiel 44:19)

As I find myself at home, having moved over streets or roads, or having moved from one room to another, or perhaps having moved only within my outlook on life, I find that I have brought with me reminders of my work. I am clothed as I was when I started out to do my day's stint.

Then I find that there is a comfort in changing garments. I put on something looser and less binding. I decide to wear that which will make me freer in my movements, something that I do not have to be careful with as I enter into the evening.

The change is as refreshing to me as the greater freedom of the less tightly designed apparel. The change signifies that I can, in a sense, say to myself, "Well done, servant, enter into rest until morning." These words remind me of similar but far more blessed words that I hope to hear when my final day's toil is finished. The change is from schedule and discipline to unmarked minutes and hours lived in informality. A patient in a hospital has this sense of relief when the doctors have gone home to be with their families and the nurse has done all that needs to be done until morning.

I have found, however, that this change into comfortable clothing means something only at the end of a well-lived day of doing my best at whatever small task God has placed before me. I must have girded myself, if only mentally and by willpower, to be a part of the tense, busy world in which I live before I can enjoy ungirding. A truant schoolboy never fully enjoys the fishing or other fun on the day he slips away from classes;

when he has an earned holiday he plays joyously.

Even the priests in the holy place lived by the rule of ministering in one set of garments which they removed after they had finished their ministry. My custom, which is the custom of most of mankind, of accepting the luxury of a change to comfortable clothes has real sense behind it; I am a changed person as I see myself in garments that are not made for a working day. My mood changes with the clothing; there is a mellowing and an anticipation of new pleasures to come.

For Difference: I sense, O Lord, that I am not made for one activity all the day long; I feel that there is a reward for labor in relaxation and freedom of movement. May I receive the full benefit of this blessing. *Amen.*

EVENING MEAL

"Whether therefore ye eat, or drink, or whatsoever ye do, do all to the glory of God." (I Corinthians 10:31)

"Why do I eat three meals a day?" I have asked myself. Breakfast, lunch, and dinner (or supper) are as much a part of the day's routine as getting up and going to bed.

Possibly the answer is that our modern industrial world demands set time periods of its employees. Or there may be the dictatorship of the body which indicates when food is needed.

In any event, I expect to have an evening meal when the activity of the day is over, and I look forward to it as an unhurried time of enjoying what is on the table. Breakfast and lunch are eaten in the shadow of responsibilities to be discharged. But dinner may be as leisurely as I wish with no sense of guilt attached.

If possible I like to take my evening meal in the company of family or friends. Good conversation and an exchange of tales of pleasant happenings during the day enrich the flavor of the food. I recall that a poet spoke of a loaf of bread eaten in the wilderness as making a paradise if there were also his beloved companion to share the simple fare. There is much truth in this.

But if I must eat alone as the world counts being alone, I may be sure of the company of the Lord. In his earthly career Jesus surrounded himself with followers, and he accepted invitations to meals where there were people to whom he could talk. Always, in a word of grace before meals, I invite him.

So I sit down to dinner and am glad. There is sheer enjoyment, but there is more. Purpose is here as it is all around me. From hour to hour I am aware that nothing is in vain. What may I learn of myself at this time?

For one thing, I know that I am eating my heartiest meal of the day because I shall not eat again for twelve hours. What nourishment I take must keep my physical mechanism running smoothly until morning. There comes to mind the biblical account of a prophet who ate one meal that had to last him for forty days and forty nights. My food need not keep me for so long, but the principle is the same.

Another thing I know is that what I am doing can be done to the glory of God. By accepting my human necessity, by patiently repeating the evening custom (perhaps 25,000 times in a lifetime!), by seeing in the homely action of eating God's provision for me, I bring glory to God.

And, last, I know that my 25,000th or 30,000th evening meal will be my last supper before I go on to sit down to the eternal table of the Lord.

For Manna: My God, I thank thee as I think of the last evening meal of our Lord, and, by faith, I realize that I can become one seated with others around that sacred board. For the sustenance that will care for me on my long journey of the night I am truly grateful. *Amen.*

TALK

"My tongue also shall talk of thy righteousness all the day long." (Psalm 71:24)

I sit down after the evening meal and find that I am in an expansive mood. Or if my movements today must be somewhat restricted, I settle back for conversation. I long for someone to talk to who will talk to me. In my memory is written the conclusion of wise men that man is more than animal because he can communicate in an intimate and minute way with his kind.

No matter how routine the day may have been, there are things that I have done and things that have been done to me that I need to review and evaluate with the help of another. Things that have haunted me are searched out and routed for the unimportant trivia that they are; my mind is freed of them. Things that at the time seemed of no consequence may become precious treasure as they are turned over in talk. The roughhewn day is shaped and smoothed by the gentle chipping and rubbing of talk. The conversation becomes my diary, and I may help prepare the diary of the other or others.

There is a question in my mind as to whether or not we may speak of talk as idle conversation. Any kind of talk is a relief of a sort, and many deep concerns are delicately brought out by indirect remarks. If my companion remarks, "This has been a pleasant day, hasn't it?" I do not brush him off for saying something obvious when I was expecting great wisdom. On the contrary I must understand that he may be wanting to assure himself that it was a good day after all, or he may be filled with some secret goodness that his day has produced. Surely the speaker has more than the weather in mind.

In my talk too I find that often the dialogue will touch upon the help of God all the day long. Nothing that has happened is purely human; the Creator has been involved at every step of the way. This must be so inasmuch as we have eternal life, and no longer can there be any separation within us into moments that are with God and moments that are without God.

If this evening I have a loved one or a friend or

a circle of companions, I am greatly blessed. But if I have no one in the room that I can see, I shall talk to my Heavenly Father just as confidently as I would to a man, woman, or child. He has promised to hear me, and I must practice for that time when the Saviour and I speak face to face.

The Goodness of Talk: My Lord, I marvel at the ability given to men to convey ideas and longings by the use of words; I am overjoyed that I am permitted the miracle of conversation with thy other children. May the words of my mouth be acceptable in thy sight. *Amen.*

READING

"The cloak that I left at Troas with Carpus, when thou comest, bring with thee, and the books, but especially the parchments." (II Timothy 4:13)

When I have eaten and talked, I find a favorite occupation that is both eating and talking—reading. A wise philosopher has said that reading makes a full man. As I read, the author of the book or article is talking to me, and I inwardly argue with or commend him.

In my books or magazines or papers I have arrested conversation; instead of floating away in the wind, the words put in print stay for years or centuries just as the writer first started them out in the world. And I may command these authors to be with me and talk with me. Family or friends may not be available, but a man or woman who has set down something which is in type never can refuse to speak to the lowliest or greatest.

My reading will be of many sorts. I may wish to move into new and exciting worlds; I may need to be reassured about this world; I may long for the rhythm of poetry after a fairly humdrum day; I may require something solid to counteract the froth of superficial happenings. Vicariously as I read I can become an adventurer, a scholar, a minstrel, a man of power, or a little child. I may discover the North Pole or be shot off in a space ship to the moon.

As I read I can understand how the apostle Paul wrote to have his books and his parchments sent to him along with his cloak. He might need the cloak in a cold, cell-like dwelling, but he needed with equal urgency the reading material that could send him forth into the expanse of God's world.

This evening, as is true of every evening, my final reading will be from the Word of God called the Bible. Here I find the lamp for my feet as darkness gathers in. The verses and the chapters tell me of God's dealing with people just as forlorn and sinful as I. Hope comes to me, and an assurance that the Lord will never leave me or forsake me. I find again and again the familiar, arrested conversation of Jesus as he walked among men. He speaks to me as I join the little band of disciples and stand shyly on the fringe of the group. By reading I take my place on mountain or seashore.

My reading today will be added to the reading of my lifetime, and it will be part of me long after the calories and vitamins of the evening meal have spent their strength.

Reading Is Life: For the joy and instruction and inspiration and experiences of reading I cannot thank thee enough, O Lord. Thou hast given me the companionship of the great and the good; thou hast enabled many to talk to me from their hearts. And for thy Holy Word, most especially, I render my praise. *Amen.*

MUSIC

"Herman and Jeduthun with trumpets and cymbals for those that should make a sound, and with musical instruments of God." (I Chronicles 16:42)

I am greedy! An evening of eating, talking, and reading should satisfy me, but I want more—I desire some music.

Just as a book or printed article seems to me as arrested conversation, talk caught in a permanent mold, music is to me the echo of my sweetest dreams and deepest longings. As I listen to music wonderful things happen to me.

For one thing, the years fall away. A martial tune reminds me of the thrill of parades watched in childhood and renews early resolves to go out and fight good battles for humanity. Love songs take me back to the age of romance when I dreamed of the person who would find me worthy of sharing a long lifetime.

Music revives in me the old faith in mankind that started me out to trust everyone and see the best in him. Once again the world is peopled with lovely princesses and handsome princes and doughty knights to right all wrongs.

Music quiets my nerves and brings a soothing feeling of

> God's in his heaven—
> All's right with the world.

From this point I am carried on to the deeply devotional music of some of the great composers of all ages who, through their symphonies, sought their Creator. I follow them to the very presence of the Eternal.

This is what music does for me time and time again. But where shall I find my music? A radio, perhaps recorded music on a record player, the simple performances of friends or neighbors, someone playing a piano nearby, the choir and organ in my church. Occasionally it may be my good fortune to go out to hear an orchestra. Once a year carolers go by my window.

Intense joy in music comes naturally to a child of God. In ancient times the priests of the Most High were encouraged to provide music for worship. The Bible contains many instances of God's people playing on various instruments. David was a musician, apparently of some real ability. In the days of Daniel music in pagan temples was the signal for the worshipers to acknowledge their god.

As I think of all this today, I realize that all my life music has been a blessing, and it moves me now particularly as evening is coming to a close.

The experience of music may be a link between this world and the next. Perhaps a great surge of melody in my soul in this world will rise to an ecstatic crescendo as I step over into that world "so bright and fair," where day and night the songs of praises are heard.

Thoughts of Music: I adore thee, O God, for all the pleasures and anticipations of this life that are sent from thee. And now as I am thinking of music I have heard, I am filled with unspeakable joy which draws me nearer to thee. *Amen.*

TO SLEEP

"When thou liest down, thou shalt not be afraid: yea, thou shalt lie down, and thy sleep shall be sweet." (Proverbs 3:24)

I find myself at the end of my day. It has been a wonderful day because I have lived. And because I have lived, I have been in turn happy and sad, filled and hungry, at ease and in pain, in company and alone. Now all that remains is to close this day with dignity and thanksgiving.

How shall I close it? In the way ordained of God—by going to sleep. After that, this day is history and memory.

In early childhood I was reluctant to go to bed and admit that a happy day was over, especially a Christmas! But now I have become accustomed to the lifelong routine and do not resist the call of weariness. I have learned that there is always a tomorrow.

I depend too upon the promise of God that when I lie down, my sleep will be sweet. Sleep is one of the richest of all God's good gifts.

My sleep will do things to this day that is past. Somehow my slumber will take the day and blow away the shadows as the sunrise drives away the mists of a foggy morning. The day will be golden, and even the flaws will be seen in their proper small perspective on the otherwise perfect surface.

If the day has brought real sorrows or losses, the sleep will take a little bit off the heavy load, and night by night the weight will be lightened a bit more.

As I sleep I have a wrestling match with the needs and hurts of mankind, and I am a changed person by morning, blessed with a new compassion.

Best of all, in sleep God gives me some foretaste of what my Lord really is, and my love for him deepens.

Of all that I have done this day, and of all that has happened to me, perhaps sleep is the truest symbolism. God gives his beloved sleep in this part of life and, at the end, the sleep of transition which we call death. At that time I can be just as ready to end this lifelong day as I am to end an ordinary day because I am just as sure that there is a tomorrow.

So I lie down and wait for sleep which will be sweet, and I trust God as to my awakening.

Before Sleep: "Now I lay me down to sleep." The old childhood prayer comes as easily to my lips, Lord, as it did of old. I rest upon the everlasting arms, awaiting thy pleasure. *Amen.*

II
Dawn . . .
until Dusk

Things which may happen to me today or tomorrow
or some day but not every day.
Surprises . . . bonuses . . . sorrows
. . . adventures.

ROUTINE BROKEN

"For we have heard him say, that this Jesus of Nazareth shall destroy this place, and shall change the customs which Moses delivered to us." (Acts 6:14)

I feel so comfortable when everything goes along according to my regular schedule! Up at the same hour every day, or cared for when I cannot get up, meals, work, leisure—all on time and in the same fashion. Routine makes me live with a feeling of security.

But when my routine is broken! How upset I am, and how hard it is to settle down to anything until my life returns to normal. I am much like the woman who sat in the same place in the church vestry every Wednesday for midweek services. One week repairs were made, and the floor was repainted where her chair always stood. When she came to the meeting and saw the situation, she fidgeted nervously, then took a chair, planted it on the repaired spot, and sat with her feet in the wet paint. She could not bear the prospect of a different pattern of action.

Why do I have this aversion to change? I think it may be because the familiar ways give me an assurance of continuity and permanence, while the strange and different calls for thought and faith and readjustment.

And yet I know that I must expect my routine to be broken often and, many times, irreparably. As a river which meets a rock or landslide that a storm has thrown into its bed must cut a new channel to its destination, so must I develop new customs and habits.

It seems possible to me when I think of this particular trait of mine that Jesus was rejected by many simply because he was suggesting some new ways of conduct beyond the instructions of Moses. When the Lord said, "You have heard that it was said . . . but I say unto you . . ." he upset the moral and spiritual routine of his listeners, and they preferred the old ways, even to the point of doing the Saviour to death.

If today my routine is to be subject to radical change, I need to remember that few adventures await me in my old ruts. I know every turn and every object on the old road. It is only on new paths that I shall meet new things and new satisfactions. My old habits make my life automatic, and I begin to live without knowing how I live.

Perhaps my greatest blessing today is that I find a big obstacle before me, and I am faced with planning a new channel for my pioneering toward the future.

In the Face of Strangeness: Lord, hold my hand. I know that I should welcome the new and different, but I am weak enough to want to hold on to the ways of my fathers which I know so well. Help me to remember that I must be ready for a new heaven and a new earth. *Amen.*

ILLNESS

"But when Jesus heard *that,* he said, This sickness is not unto death, but for the glory of God, that the Son of God might be glorified thereby." (John 11:4)

I do not feel well today. An illness has taken hold of me. I am a bit panic-stricken. When an injury, a germ, a virus, an inner obstruction brings pain or discomfort, I do not know what the outcome will be.

Perhaps it is the uncertainty as much as the discomfort that is bothering me. Will I recover at all? If I do, will I be handicapped permanently or for a long time? Is life as I know it now to be only a memory from this time on?

Of course, I tell myself, I am bound in the bundle of life with all the world, and I must expect to take my share of the misfortunes of mankind.

But must this illness of mine be a misfortune? Is there not some way I can turn this discomfiture to profit? The enforced inactivity could be useful for planning for future work, for reading, for setting an example to others of assurance in a time of distress, for prayer and inner growth.

Certainly I know one thing—this illness is not unto death. No matter what may happen to me, this is bound to be true since there is no death. After the illness has had its course, I shall live in this world or in the better world. I find that this knowledge calms the panic, and I begin to accept the sickness and set myself to fight it.

I remember that someone said, "You are tougher than you think." I find this to be true. I can stand the pain or numbness. I can reconcile myself to being apart from my usual pursuits and companions.

Also, I begin to understand the suffering of the world, for I too have been considered worthy to be one with all sufferers. I sense that never again can I be the same indifferent, half-sympathetic person that I was when I visited the sick and tried to cheer them up.

Today warns me of my mortality. This illness may well be temporary and leave no scars, but it prepares me for the time when God will call and I shall answer.

In the meantime of my illness the Heavenly Father seems nearer to me than ever, for I hasten to open the door for him.

Finding Myself Unwell: This seems not to be myself, O Lord. What has happened? Have I failed in the commonsense of eating, working, relaxing? Or have I simply paid the price for being in the

world close to my weak fellowman? Make me
know how this illness may refine and purify me.
Amen.

HOLIDAYS

"And in every province and in every city, where-
ever the king's command and his edict came, there
was gladness and joy among the Jews, a feast and
a holiday." (Esther 8:17 RSV)

I awake today with a cheerful outlook on life,
for this is not an ordinary day with ordinary ex-
pectations; it is a holiday.

In a real sense a holiday is a holy day to me.
I count over the holidays and find they all are for
the purpose of remembering some great event of
the past. There is the Fourth of July to bring to
mind the birth of our nation; there is Thanksgiving to commemorate the first harvest of a starving
people in this new world; there is Memorial Day

to honor the men and women who have given their lives for our freedom; there is Christmas, the day selected to represent the birthday of our Lord. Every holiday has been bought for us by great men and women or by great and selfless deeds.

And so I prepare to be glad and sober: glad for the restfulness and festivities of the day, sober in thinking of the origin of this day.

So often I have thought of holidays as times of recreation. And so they are if the accent is correctly placed on re-creation. Cessation from my customary work and goings and comings will refresh my body; a use of the available leisure will refresh my mind; a review of the reasons behind this holiday will renew my soul.

My holiday can become a lock in the canal of my life. I have seen a boat come up a canal to a lock and the gates close securely behind it. Water poured into the compartment where the boat waited, raising it to a higher level. Then the gate in front opened and the boat was received on the new level. And so on until the voyage was continued far above the original altitude. I think of this holiday in that way. It can raise me to a higher level for continuing my living above the things of the past.

In the book of Esther I read today that where the king's commands came, there was feasting and a holiday. If I pause before my out-of-school mood gets the better of me, I shall realize that when the commands of the King of kings come, there is always feasting and a holy day. The early Christians rejoiced with exceeding great joy. After the Resurrection the believers displayed the holiday spirit continually. They had the King's commands to cast all their care on him and be anxious for nothing.

My holiday parts the Red Sea of my turbulent life, and this day I shall go across the sea bed unassailed.

For Extra Days: O Lord, I like my holidays chiefly because they seem as bonuses in the succession of mornings and evenings, extra days not needed for the laboring of thy children. May I savor this day and profit by it. *Amen.*

BEREAVEMENT

"And God shall wipe away all tears from their eyes; and there shall be no more death." (Revelation 21:4)

I have come face to face with death today. My soul is shaken within me.

Now I know above all that I am one with all mankind. What person is there who has not lost a father, a mother, child, brother, sister, friend? Who has not or will not weep disconsolately, as I do, for one who was and is not? This day I have joined that great company of mourners.

The loved face, the welcome voice cannot be found again in any corridor of this world. There is silence and absence.

What is the true source of my grief?

I ask, am I sorry for the dear person who has died, or am I sorry for myself?

Perhaps I do cry for that one. Perhaps I regret with an agonizing pity that life had not been kinder, that the road had not been smoother, that greater acclamation had not been awarded, that so much hoped for and planned for had to be left unrealized and undone.

Yes, I do grieve for the life now come to a full stop. That silent one will never again play on the chords of a sweet life to sound forth to the world notes of sorrow, of joy, of exultation, of love. Only echoes are left.

But in honesty I admit to myself that the larger share of my mourning is selfish. This death has affected *me*. *I* am left and bereft.

Perhaps I am sorry for myself that I have lost the love and assurance that kept me going when all the world seemed against me. Perhaps I dread the rift in my placid existence. It may be that I begrudge rest to the hands and feet that ministered to me in one way or another. As a mother said when her child's fatal accident was reported to her, "What will become of *me*? What shall *I* do now?" Subconsciously, even though I fight against the temptation, *my* loss is being assessed even while I think I am suffering for the victim of disease or accident.

And there is the pain of my guilt. I could have been more considerate; I might have made life more joyful; there were loving words I could have said. Oh, if I had just one more day how different would be my attitude toward my beloved!

I need to listen to God, and I do listen. I hear that for God's children there is no death. I am made confident that the world beyond is real while this is at best a feverish prelude. My remorse is assuaged in knowing that God is greater than my accusing heart and God does not condemn me. I am taught to recognize that the love and friendship of the one taken is my proof that I am not the self-centered person that I have been conjuring up.

I am bereaved today, and my ties to this world are less desperate and taut. I look forward to the place where there is no more death. In patience, but with an unafraid anticipation, I await my Lord's call to me also.

When Death Appears: My Lord, this day has shaken me. And I turn to thee as the only unshakable person in all my world. Give me understanding of what has happened to my loved one and to me. *Amen.*

JOY

"Weeping may endure for a night, but joy cometh in the morning." (Psalm 30:5)

I am not sure why, but I am filled with joy this morning.

And I have found, through the years, that joy may be of two kinds. One variety is like a boy bouncing a ball. He seems unable to stop; he bounces and bounces his ball in sheer abandon. For the moment his whole world is in motion.

My joy has something of that feeling today. Everything seems buoyant. Nothing is static and staid. I know now how the Old Testament writer felt when he mentioned the mountains skipping like rams and the hills like lambs. All the affairs of my life have a gaiety and variety.

Too, I feel the other kind of joy that is like heat therapy. It is the contentment of the body exposed to the warm rays of the sun. I sense a healing seeping through my whole being.

Joy can be like this, I know. Some warmth from the Eternal touches soul and body, and there is a restfulness and soothing that is hard to describe.

All things good seem possible, and the little petty annoyances of life are no more distracting than so many crickets chirping nearby.

Mysterious is the coming of joy. It comes not always when things are going well, and sometimes when life is not smooth at all. A day such as this day of joy comes and goes as the wind without warning or notice.

I accept the joy today and I do not seek to analyze it. I remember that joy is contagious. Perhaps I have caught it from someone; certainly I intend to expose myself to others hoping that some may "take" my condition and be joyful too.

While I am feeling a little bit guilty that I have this slightly giddy state of being, I remember for my peace of mind that I am commanded to be joyful. Everything about my faith points to joy. Fear, anxiety, hopelessness, despair kill joy, but these doleful thoughts have been done away by the triumphant life of my Lord.

Before my joy I was like a person pinned down by a landslide. I was at the point of suffocation until someone came and lifted the oppressive weight, shovel by shovel. My landslide was brought on by my unbelief, and the Saviour came to lift my burdens off one by one until I stood free. This standing free and unhampered is joy.

Today I am filled with joy unspeakable and full of glory.

While Rejoicing: Gladness, O Lord, is my gift to thee this day. May I remember that I am to come before thee ever with thanksgiving and a song. *Amen.*

THE BLUES

"Why art thou cast down, O my soul? and why art thou disquieted in me? hope thou in God; for I shall yet praise him for the help of his countenance." (Psalm 42:5)

What is the matter with me today? I see everything as though it were covered with a heavy layer of dust. Nothing seems worth the seeing or the handling. My mind is as beclouded as my eyes. Nothing but dismal thoughts will come. Nothing seems certain except that I am a complete failure.

Why do I have the blues?

I can think of nothing that has happened to plunge me into gloom. There have been other occasions when disappointments, losses, and stupid mistakes have not brought me to such a low state as I find myself in today. Why?

Weariness may have something to do with my condition. Possibly I have pushed myself beyond whatever strength or endurance is mine at the present time. Perhaps the infinitely wise physical system given me by God has thrown into my bloodstream substances that will slow me down so that I will not go to the point of complete break.

Or I may have been "running on the battery," as automobile men say of a car that is getting no power from the gasoline fuel. In this condition I may have failed to notice that my necessary tie with the source of power had broken and I was strictly on my own weak substitute. And, just as a battery will eventually be run down, my unaided exertions will fail to keep me going. And the blues result.

I ask myself if this is what happened to the psalmist who wondered why he was so cast down and disquieted? He saw only one way out of his despond; he reminded himself to "hope in God."

I do not know for sure why I have the blues. Perhaps one of the two reasons given is my explanation, or there may be another less obvious. All I know is that I am miserable.

And when I am miserable I know only the answer of the writer of old: hope in God. The Lord has delivered me before, and he will now. My cheerfulness will return and my interest in this wonderful world and the fascinating people in it.

Before long I shall be able to sing praises to the Most High, and thank him for bringing me out of this distress. This very thought is already putting the gloom to flight.

In Discontent: O Lord, thou knowest the faults of men that they depend on the outward so much that they forget to care for the inward being. Relieve my strange burden and let me, again, rest back on the everlasting arms. *Amen.*

VISITORS

"Now when Job's three friends heard of all this evil that was come upon him, they came every one from his own place." (Job 2:11)

I heard a knock on my door today, and when I opened the door I found that I had visitors. That is a blessed word, visitors.

Callers were especially welcome today because, unwittingly, I had placed myself in solitary confinement. Due to preoccupation, carelessness, or lack of confidence in my ability to offer anything of value to my fellowman, occasionally I withdraw from social life.

Solitary confinement has been found by prison keepers to be the worst punishment that can be inflicted on anyone. Enforced loneliness is more than can be borne over a period of time.

But when visitors come they reestablish my happy relationship with other people. They break down the bars of my self-made cell, and I am released to share my deepest longings with others. My visitors talk to me and I to them. To strangers this conversation might seem inconsequential— small talk. But I am convinced that there is no such thing as small talk. All talk is communication and keeps open the floodgates of the mind.

My visitors ask, "How have you been?" And we inquire about families and mutual friends, the books we have read and letters received. We share our burdens, and each one takes part of the load carried by the other, until the troubles are so light that they can be carried with ease.

Visitors come to me for many reasons or no reason, but I can be sure that they will come when they hear that some ill has befallen me.

Just as Job's three friends came each from his own place when they heard of Job's misfortunes, so my friends hasten to my side if there is bad news of me.

Our Lord made much of the duty of men to visit the sick and those in prison and said that such visits were as though made to him.

After my visitors left today, I determined to do my best to stay out of solitary confinement, and I resolved that when illness or other handicaps put me in the cell against my choice I will calm my soul, knowing that visitors will come soon. And if no one else came, I would confidently expect a visitation from God.

From Prison: Heavenly Father, I thank thee for the ordinary, unassuming men, women, and young people who are my visitors in days of joy or sorrow. Particularly, I am indebted to thy love that visits me regularly. *Amen.*

TRIPS

"He went out from thence, and came into his own country." (Mark 6:1)

I am going somewhere today. I have a trip to make. This may prove to be exciting and stimulating.

In the first place, the trip will pry me loose from where I am. There is a tendency with me to fasten onto my present residence like a barnacle, and I must exert real will power to let go of the location I know so well. This is good of itself because there will come a time when I must release my grip on what the apostle Paul called "this present world."

Another thing the trip will do for me is to offer a change of scene. I have looked at my own room or rooms, the pictures on the walls, my possessions in their familiar spots until I do not see vividly the good or beauty of my surroundings. Familiarity may not have bred contempt, but it has brought on indifference. New sights and sounds and faces may not be superior, but they will be strange enough to command close attention. My faculties will receive some much needed exercise.

Further, the trip will disclose the pot of gold at the end of some rainbow. Journey's end may be in the home of a beloved relative or friend; it may be in a gathering of people discussing some important subject of religion, art, or social affairs; it may be at a shrine to which I have made pilgrimage—a shrine of childhood haunts, a school attended years ago, a cemetery. Something of gold awaits. The treasure may be memory, learning, renewed acquaintance, love. In some way the trip will be rewarding.

The manner of my trip may be walking or traveling by bus, train, automobile, airplane; or it may be simply in the imagination of my mind. If I am physically unable to do other than let my mind go without the rest of me, I shall find that this brings the same profit as a more mobile trip.

In the New Testament I find many instances of trips made by Jesus. At least once he started out from one place and came to his own country. This can be true of my trip today. Despite my reluctance to pull loose from present quarters and present thoughts, I have an inner feeling of being a transient lodger here. My country must be elsewhere, beyond the far horizon. If I have the courage to make trips, I shall find much evidence of who I am and where I belong. In the last analysis I must say with Augustine, "I am restless until I rest in God."

As a Voyager: O Thou who art always at the end of any trip, either actual or in the kingdom of the mind, bring me to a happy place with good comrades. Help me to understand what I am to see and hear. *Amen.*

WORSHIP

"O come, let us worship and bow down: let us kneel before the Lord, our Maker! For he is our God; and we are the people of his pasture, and the sheep of his hand." (Psalm 95:6-7)

Worship is part of each of my days, but today I am drawn to a closer examination and experience of this essential part of life.

I find that worship is an approach to God. Not that God is far from me, but I sense that the decision to draw near is mine. And I am only moved to come when I am aware of my deep need for my Creator. Worship is an urgency within me. I have no choice but to seek out the source of my being.

My worship may be solitary today, as many times it must be, but if I can find another seeker, or several, or many seekers, I shall find the joint adoration greatly uplifting. There is an obedience in gathering together that repays the worshipers. The Lord is there with the two or three or more.

What shall I expect of my worship today? The years have taught me to look for a mutuality. The spirit of the Lord meets with my spirit, and there is communication and fellowship of that part of me which is the image of God, with God. I am "surprised by joy" as I know that I am loved by my Heavenly Father. And this while I know myself to be utterly unworthy. The nearer I come to the Lord my Maker, the surer I am that there is nothing I can bring as a trophy for which I could feel free to expect to be favored. God's love is a free grace.

Knowing that pride has no part in worship, I remember that worshipers through the ages have thought of bowing and kneeling as expressive of an inner obeisance. Of course I realize that the physical posture has no bearing on worship unless it is truly symbolic of what I am feeling in my heart. Arrogance that bows can become humility, and pride that kneels can become self-yielding.

One thing that I cannot demand of worship today is perfection. After my special moments of drawing close to the Creator, I find that I am the same sinner moved by the same earthy desires and intrigued by the same temptations. And yet I shall be changed; I shall abhor that which is evil in me, and I shall reach out for the good as never before.

Each experience of worship ennobles me to some extent and sharpens my ability to know what is becoming to a child of God.

Today I forgo minor things in order to engage in the major occupation of an immortal soul—I seek the kingdom and righteousness by worship.

In Worship: O Lord my Maker, I know that I have fallen far short of thy glory. But nothing is impossible with thee. I have failed as a child—make me as a hired servant that I may always be near thee. *Amen.*

ACHIEVEMENT

"So Solomon built the house, and finished it." (I Kings 6:14)

I have achieved today!
After months of chipping away, I now see the

final and worthy result standing out in pure outline from the marble block of my solid toil. Often
I was ready to quit; day after day the little I did
seemed so futile and useless that there was no
incentive to keep on. My life was being wasted, I
thought.

But now, today, I can stand back and say that
the product of my agonizing application to the
labor is good. In a reverent sense I understand
how it was with God at the creation, when he
looked upon his handiwork and found it good.
Perhaps this is evidence that I am in the image of
God. I need to make and to do and to be. In my
limited way I too must create.

And I know there is a penalty to this heritage.
The hunger to achieve is never appeased. What
I see today as something accomplished will not
satisfy for long. There must be more and other
achievements. Always there must be something
that expresses the best of my skill whether of hand
or brain, finished or in progress.

In progress—that must be the secret. Achievement is more in the doing than in the finishing.
Today I realize that my joy in looking upon my
trophy is in knowing that all along I have been

achieving and my days have not been in vain; I have added something to the world.

Being imperfect, I know that I shall indulge myself in at least a brief period of self-adulation; I shall stand back and look at what I have done; I shall be tempted to tell others to come and see or hear; I shall say to myself, "Well done, thou good and faithful servant."

And I think that this little lapse from worthwhile effort may be good for me. It may bring a new desire to achieve yet more, since the reward in joy of having carried something of worth to its final solution is sweet.

Today I feel a kinship to Solomon, who built God's house and finished it. I have more than a vague conviction that every good and decent thing I achieve will be adding to and ornamenting God's house if by faithful discipline I finish what God has gifted me to do.

In the Glow of Achievement: Lord, I know that everything I have been able to do or think is by the grace which comes only from thee. And this achievement of mine today gives me a sense of worth established forever. I thank thee, O my God. *Amen.*

MEMORY

"I remember the days of old; I meditate on all thy works; I muse on the work of thy hands." (Psalm 143:5)

Today I have come to the sure knowledge of something that has been endeavoring to get my attention for a long time—I possess the greatest treasure in the world!

When I think of this treasure I am not evaluating by comparison with the diamond mines of Kimberley, the gold of Fort Knox, the crown jewels of the old empires, pirate loot, or the wealth of the oil deposits in the earth. These are childish baubles compared to my riches.

My wealth is memory.

Today I realize suddenly that I have an inexhaustible storehouse from which I can draw endlessly.

Packed away in memory's vaults are all the precious little events of childhood, the delicious dreams of early youth, the small virtues of young adulthood, the responsible parts played up until now.

In memory I find love, chastening sorrow, failures that ended in later victory, life filed away in indestructible form. The years gone by are preserved for reruns at my pleasure.

Unhappily I find all things are retained, not only the pleasant and happy events and words and thoughts. This, of course, is a wise provision, or I would not learn from the past and be warned to avoid the sins and mistakes of my earlier days. I might be so proud of my expurgated career that I would be prone to fall into traps in the present.

My example as I open the door of my memory closet is the psalmist who thought of the days of old only to meditate on the mighty works of God. As the panorama of my years turns slowly in my mind, I can see now, as I could not see then, that at every moment of every one of my days the Lord was standing by me and turning even my errors into some profit for me. How many times he has kept my feet from falling and my eyes from tears!

I am aware today also that my memory needs a good housecleaning once in a while just as my room or my desk does. I have kept too many things and too many of the wrong things. As one wise writer put it, memory is like a demented witch treasuring up bits of rags and straws and other trash instead of the real gems of life. The trash of resentment, remembered injury and insult, of suspicion and imagined wrongs, I will clean out to make room for all that has been pure and just and lovely. If God cannot remember my transgressions, neither shall I remember the misguided deeds of others.

In the Grip of Memory: O Lord, my memory is spilling out things old and new today. I am humbled at what I see of myself, and yet I rejoice at the thousands of blessed remembrances—all made meaningful by thee. *Amen.*

AGING

"I have been young, and now am old; yet I have not seen the righteous forsaken, nor his seed begging bread." (Psalm 37:25)

"The righteous . . . still shall bring forth fruit in old age." (Psalm 92:12-14)

I received an unwelcome and violent shock today.

"There is nothing wrong with you," said the doctor, "except that you must accept the fact that you are no longer as young as you were."

Am I actually old? Aging, the statisticians say, starts quite early. Industries look carefully at a prospective employee of thirty-eight or older.

But, I complain to myself, others get old; I am active and energetic. I look at least fifteen years younger than I am!

Indeed, the years have passed away as imperceptibly as snowflakes melting in the sun. Where has life gone?

There it is, though. The doctor has told me; my

friends know it but won't mention it; my mirror is honest—yes, I am aging.

All right. How different am I from the person I was ten years ago?

In the first place, I insist that aging is not a total condition. My body is bound to show the results of the warfare of years. No one can escape this circumstance. Indeed, who would not choose to keep an appearance compatible with his contemporaries?

Age of the mind, however, is optional. If I continue to show a vital interest in people and events, if I read as much as I am able, if I am challenged to try new things, if I keep as active physically as is wise, then I can expect mental youth.

Age of my emotional person is optional also. Rigidity of response, intolerance of new things, a negative reaction as a normal condition could bring on aging.

These are the things I am saying to myself today. I insist that my aging is conditional and partial. I intend to fight back and refuse to be obsolete.

And I have help in my struggle. The years of my life have shown me that the righteous is never forsaken, and I have the promise that the righteous will bring forth fruit in his old age.

What then is the fear of aging if I am to be permitted to add something to the world even as when I was young? My daily schedule may be a bit constricted and limited, but it may be by God's help far more satisfying than my earlier scattered efforts.

In Years: My Father, I remember that thou hast been called the Ancient of Days, the First and the Last. Since I began with thee, I am content to end with thee. Thou hast the key to eternal youth. *Amen.*

MOVING

"Now the Lord had said unto Abram, Get thee out of thy country, and from thy kindred, and from thy father's house, unto a land that I will shew thee." (Genesis 12:1)

Today I must pull up roots.

This is about the last thing I wanted to do. I have been satisfied here. I do not want to move.

But circumstances make it advisable that I change my residence.

I have moved before, and it is always sad at first. My familiar neighborhood is left behind. Grocers, mailmen, newsboys are new and unknown. Friends are at a distance, and I must find others. My furniture looks older and shabbier in the new quarters.

Even so, I must move and be one of the millions who will be pulling up roots and faring forth to strange and untried communities this day.

It seems that as the world grows older, its people are forced to live more and more as pilgrims. Industry calls its men and women with siren offers of good jobs and more money. Political decisions and city rebuilding plans dislodge great groups of people. Economic conditions require the seeking of smaller and cheaper rooms or houses.

But, no matter what the reason, moving must be faced. Plans must be made.

There is the problem of discarding unnecessary possessions. To my surprise I find that I have been a great collector. Each article has been "much too good" to throw away. Keepsakes, things needing repair, old greeting cards, files of magazines. Every piece has a memory; why not take every-thing? Because room in the moving van is at a premium, and expenses must be pared. I give away and throw away until my belongings are in a manageable amount.

The rest is routine—the packing, the marking, the weariness, the wondering about this decision, or the regrets over mistakes that brought on the necessity for the move, perhaps.

And then I think of Abram. He went much farther than I am to go. He left his country and went out to a strange land, not knowing where he was going. But one thing he knew—he was going at the command of God, and God would show him the land, a promised land.

This move of mine is not unknown to God. I am as much his child as Abram was. Before me is an unfamiliar place, but God will show me the land which is to be my promised land. This will serve to remind me that in this world I have no continuing city, and wherever I am, God will be also.

On the Move: I am no better than my fathers, Lord, who left security to find freedom and opportunity in a new world. May I have the same spirit of adventure and the same desire to seek thee. *Amen.*

CATASTROPHES

"Or those eighteen, upon whom the tower in Siloam fell, and slew them, think ye that they were sinners above all men that dwelt in Jerusalem?" (Luke 13:4)

Disaster has befallen me today. At least, from my human standpoint, I call it a disaster.

One of those happenings called, strangely enough, "acts of God" has occurred to me.

And, like several of my friends who have had similar catastrophes in their lifetimes, I am immediately asking, "Why me? What have I done to deserve this?" Without wishing harm to anyone, I can name several flagrant sinners who might be more likely victims if victims there had to be.

I find catastrophes hard to understand. The risk of earthquakes, tidal waves, fires started by lightning, great and damaging storms is added to the many misfortunes I may bring upon myself. Is not life hazardous enough without these extra dangers?

In my anguish I turn to God for an answer. I

search the Bible. One illustration in the Gospel of Luke gives me a hint. The account concerns some people who were in or near a tower in Siloam and were killed because that tower fell on them.

It seems that the witnesses of this tragedy and others who heard of it jumped to the conclusion that the dead were great transgressors who deserved their fate.

Jesus, however, denied the conclusion and said that those people were not more sinful than others in the city.

At least, then, I can console myself today in the sure knowledge that I am not to blame for the damage and loss that has come to me and possibly to others near and dear to me. I happened to be in a certain place at a certain time, and just there and then the catastrophe struck. The catastrophe was not lying in wait for me or anyone; it was the inevitable result of unchanging laws in the universe.

Thinking of these laws reminds me of a man who tried to be brave about everything. When misfortunes occurred he would say, "Well, I was here first." With that bit of philosophy he would go out quite jauntily into whatever storm had befallen. Now I wonder if his attitude was the one to take?

As a matter of fact, neither he nor I were here first. The created world and planets and stars were here before man, and God had set them in motion in obedience to laws. If these laws did not work consistently—if, for instance, the law of gravity had been suspended for a moment at Siloam—all the delicate mechanism of the creation might be ruined and our universe break up around us.

But God was here first. And I am sure he knows what has happened to me today. He will help me bear this load.

In Great Dismay: O my Lord, this awesomely destructive thing has brushed me in its passing. My injury is very great. Grant me understanding, take from me any tendency to bitterness, give me hope for tomorrow. *Amen.*

GIVING

"I have shewed you all things, how that so labour-ing ye ought to remember the words of the Lord Jesus, how he said, It is more blessed to give than to receive." (Acts 20:35)

I am parting with something today.

Which is to say that I am about to give some-thing to someone. I have found that giving always involves losing. Whenever I make a gift I am de-pleted in one way or another. My pocketbook is thinner, my possessions are fewer, my strength is less, or my time is shorter. I cannot give of what I have in money, objects, effort, or hours without feeling some sense of loss. The Old Testament king knew this when he refused to give to God something that belonged to someone else; he said that he could not offer to God that which had cost him nothing.

This king had found the secret of giving which I have found. If the gift costs me nothing, I am simply at the point of transfer and not of giving.

For this reason, now that I am at the point of giving today, I am not deceiving myself into thinking that what I am doing is a trivial thing. I am not a trivial creation; I am a child of God. Every part of me has some eternal significance and the giving of myself must be in all seriousness.

Even so, I find that giving is much easier than getting. When I give I make a decision to part with something of my own, but when I receive I am in the involuntary position of accepting a part of another person, and I have the great responsibility of using what comes to me so that I shall not waste him or her.

There have been times when I have toyed with the idea of not giving, since giving imposes on the receiver such a heavy duty. But then I find that I must give. I have read with great soberness the plight of the Dead Sea that is stagnant and non-life-giving because it keeps all that comes into it. If I do not give, I find that I am stifling in the abundance that God has bestowed upon me. For my own health I must give and give and give. At the same time I must be ready to receive, since all my brothers and sisters in the world have the same necessity for giving. And, suddenly, I discover that giving is what makes mankind one great family. When I give to my neighbor a part of me, he is a part of me; when I accept from him part of him, I become part of him.

Today I have come to the conclusion that the way to "become one" as Jesus prayed that his followers might be one is to give without ceasing.

At the Parting with Myself: My Father, needy people lack what I have to give; may I give in humility and not in pride or self-esteem. And help me to know that I also am a needy person. I had a need which only thy gift of the Saviour could satisfy. I have needs that only my fellowman can supply. *Amen.*

BILLS

"Owe no man anything, but to love one another: for he that loveth another hath fulfilled the law." (Romans 13:8)

Today the time has come to pay what I owe.

This is not the kind of day that is the most welcome of all days. Indeed, I rather dread this day in the month. For there are the bills, a big stack of them. It seems that many people have done many things for me. Sadly I realize that it is easier to buy things or contract for services than it is to settle the account at the end of the week or month. I sympathize with the man in the New Testament who was seized by the throat as his creditor shouted, "Pay what thou owest!" My bills have me by the throat, as it were, and are demanding payment. I have no choice; I must pay. Even though I may need to economize and do without things for a while, I must satisfy the demands.

My pile of bills, however, can be discharged with money. There are some bills that come to me that call for a deeper and dearer payment. Extravagantly I have expended my strength in the days of my youth, and now I receive bills that demand a lessening of the pace and a doing without some of my choice pursuits. I must pay. Unwisely I have entered into friendships or family relationships on the impulse of a moment, and now I have the long bills which require making the best of what the companions I have chosen demand of me. There have been sins and acts of foolishness, and I have been lulled into thinking these quick pleasures were free; now across the years the bills come in.

The food consumed was delicious when I was eating; now the grocer needs his money. The room or house has been a snug, secure shelter from the weather; now the landlord or taxgatherer is here with his hand out. The fuel was good to cook my meals or heat my dwelling; now the electric company or gas company representative expects recompense.

All life, I find, exacts dues along the way. Some bills are submitted daily, some monthly, and some after decades, but the bills will come eventually. And I am called upon to pay as gladly as I enjoyed the good things that came to me. There are some bills, however, that I need not have had. From these that are in the number on my desk today I hope that I shall gain wisdom and true repentance; I pray that I may guard my actions and my words more carefully hereafter.

In any event, a bill calls for payment. I have

been taught to owe no one anything except *love*. This is a bill which I can only hope to pay on the installment plan. And I would not have this otherwise. To pay that bill brings me the greatest joy that I can experience.

Paying Up: Lord, thou knowest my physical needs that bring to me the bills in their season. Help me to provide the money to keep myself honest in the eyes of the world. And help me pay the bills that other men rarely see, but which are open to thine eyes. Especially help with my bill of love. *Amen.*

LOVELY THINGS

"Finally, brethren, whatsoever things are true, whatsoever things are honest, whatsoever things are just, whatsoever things are pure, whatsoever things are lovely, whatsoever things are of good report; if there be any virtue, and if there be any praise, think on these things." (Philippians 4:8)

I have a strange set of feelings today—happiness and inferiority. The reason for this contradictory state of mind is that I have seen a lovely thing in this world in which I live. The sight of this lovely thing has made me happy, but the knowledge of what true loveliness is has made me feel inferior when I examine myself.

There is this hope, however, that there must be some loveliness in me or I would not be able to separate the fair from the foul, the good from the evil, beauty from ugliness. Something in that lovely sunrise or sunset, tree or flower, face or form, harmony or cadence must be calling to something imbedded deep in my being. I remember that a poet said beauty lies in the eyes of the beholder.

If this is true today—that what I am admiring is lovely only because it seems lovely to me— where did I get this kind of judgment? How do I know but what there are people who would call beautiful the things I call ugly, and ugly the things which move me to awe? And who is right?

This puzzling thought brings me back to pondering the deeds of the Creator. It seems to me that I am on safe ground when I find the handiwork of the Almighty unspoiled by man lovely, while I protest the ugliness in the slag heaps and polluted streams which are symbolic of the distortions and commercializations springing from man's sin and greed. The face of a person who has lived close to God and who has loved his fellowman sincerely is more beautiful to me than the face of a self-indulgent, dissipated, or brutal individual.

Today, then, I think that if beauty lies in my eyes, it must have been the gift of my Maker when he was pleased to make me in his image. Any real loveliness within, which is my compass directing me to the magnificent sights and sounds in my daily reach, must be part of that small speck of eternity with which I came into the world.

As a further proof that I know what is truly lovely, I find that the sight or hearing of something which is beautiful to me turns me again to the one of whom such terms have been used as the Fairest Among Ten Thousand, the Bright and Morning Star, the Altogether Lovely—my Saviour.

Beholding Loveliness: My Father, thou hast done so much that seems beyond the necessities of life. I thank thee for all the beauty that is available to the sons of men. Most of all I thank thee that I have been made to know what is lovely and of good report. *Amen.*

LEARNING

"The wise man will hear, and will increase learning." (Proverbs 1:5)

Today I learned something.

I am quite pleased with myself because I know more than I did when I got up this morning. I know the why of something that before was hidden from me. It seems almost unbelievable that my possession of a few new facts has changed a great mystery to a simple thing.

And this realization has caused me to think of my first ancestor. How many mysteries he had, and how much to learn, and how well he did his job!

Under the ground beneath his feet were all the natural resources of oil, coal, minerals, and gems. There, unknown to him, was unleashed power, tool material, heat.

On the seashore over the hill was the sand that could be made into glass and lenses in telescope and microscope and camera.

Within his reach were trees that were potential houses and schools, and the substance for paper that could be used for books.

As my ancestor sat on a rock and looked around in awe, everything was mystery. For him and his children for countless generations was the task of learning and reducing the mysteries one by one.

Indeed, what I learned today was due to the patient discoveries of men and women before me —and I was about to be proud!

I suppose, though, that I should be entitled to a feeling of satisfaction, for I have carried on the necessary tradition of man. If I refuse to learn, I am slowing up the pushing back of the frontiers of ignorance.

This must have been part of the task that the

Creator set men when he commanded them to name the creatures and subdue the earth. My dictionary shows how well things have been named, and the power represented by electricity in my room indicates the extent of the subduing. All speak of learning.

However, I ask myself: What is the purpose of the learning? Is it just for the sake of penetrating the secrets of the universe?

But this, in a way, would be a childish pursuit, fun or a sort of hobby. And this could never be what God intended. I must think that because the Lord is truth I come nearer to him as I learn the marvels of what he has done and made. His ways appear then to be so much higher than my ways, and his thoughts so much greater than my thoughts. I am no longer wise in my own conceits.

My learning of today begins to take on new importance, and I realize that I can never learn so much that I can say I have fathomed the last mystery of God. Another thought that stays with me is, if I am following God's command in my learning, the things I have learned cannot be lost when I die. This is another proof of a more abundant life to come.

In Joy of Learning: O Thou who art the fountain of all knowledge and all wisdom; the way, the truth, and the life; I thank thee for the privilege of learning. May I increase in humility before the immensity of what I know not. *Amen.*

NEW CLOTHES

"But the father said to his servants, Bring forth the best robe, and put it on him; and put a ring on his hand, and shoes on his feet." (Luke 15:22)

Was I extravagant today? I bought something new to wear.

A garment had begun to show signs of wear and, worst of all, it had begun to take on my shape. No matter how carefully it was hung up, or how often it was pressed or cleaned, it fell into the lines of my form.

I suppose this is the chief reason I bought new clothes today. I wanted something that would resist me and give me a new outline.

analyses of the human mind. I am told that basically I am a person of violence, lust, and uncontrollable egotism. If this is true, I fear that I may do something against my lifetime pattern and will. Can I trust myself?

Too, my body may be a veritable volcano. Books and articles describe how vulnerable I am. Arteries may be at the breaking point, my heart may give out at any time, or there may be cancer!

I am full of fear.

Fear of what may happen, or of what has happened that will soon be disclosed.

How shall I rid myself of this dread? Partly by reason, but mostly without reason has my condition been brought on. Can it be conquered in the same way?

Reason does little good. Reading books of good thoughts seldom budges my fears.

I turn to God and hear again, "Fear not, for I am with thee." Only this promise helps me. If God is with me, the God of all creation, the God of all power, the conqueror of death, the forgiver of sins, of what shall I be afraid?

Now I find that my fear is of fear. For fear

Undoubtedly I am in line with everyone from Adam and Eve down to the present when I look about for clothing. Raiment makes such a change in a person. It brings a sense of newness, almost like a New Year dawning. And it brings a challenge.

For instance, I have found that if I buy a new coat I am careful to keep my shoes shined and my other clothing in good condition. In fact, the purchase of one piece of wearing apparel often calls for the buying of several others so that a new thing will not be shamed by shabby companions.

The father of the prodigal son knew this secret of the strange transforming power of new clothes. The poor, ashamed, disgraced, and almost hopeless young man was suddenly covered by the best robe in the father's house. It is safe to assume that he made his habits and entire way of life conform to the cleanliness and value of the outer garment.

In my life I have found new incentives toward the bettering of my efforts and motives because friends, loved ones, teachers, children have somehow put new garments of worth, affection, and trust upon me. How could I walk around in second-rate character and pursuits when I had been trusted with someone's best robe?

Perhaps I have not been extravagant today after all. Perhaps new clothes are not a luxury in any event. There comes a time when I must have a strong reason to pull up my relaxed resolves and self-respect.

In the New Testament I read that I may be clothed with garments of righteousness and, in the life to come, I shall walk forth a new person in my best robe.

For New Clothes: O Lord, I find myself inwardly shabby. I pray for the best robe always available for thy prodigal sons. *Amen.*

FEAR

"Fear thou not; for I am with thee: be not dismayed; for I am thy God: I will strengthen thee; yea, I will help thee, I will uphold thee with the right hand of my righteousness." (Isaiah 41:10)

I am filled with fear today.

I have a dismal premonition that something I have done is about to catch up with me, bringing disgrace or injury.

As when I was a child, I am afraid in the dark. In the shadows there are unknown and unseeable things which, because they are unknown and unseeable, are terrible.

And even though I have lived through many nights, and even though I have found that each morning brought light which showed that there were no terrors in the corners at all, I have the same quaking fear as of old.

Remembering many other days of blackness that were made unbearable simply because of m[y] imagination. I tell myself that my fear is utter[ly] inexcusable. I remind myself that the things [I] have most feared have been those that never ha[p]pened.

But still I am full of fear.

The papers are filled with predictions of w[ar,] famines, disease, crime, and other possible ca[tas]trophes. Any of these things may descend [upon] me and mine.

And, worse, magazines and books are filled

demonstrates my lack of faith in what my Heavenly Father has said.

I will have fear again, I know. But I also know the cure. I need only stop in my anguish, reach out to the Lord who is ever near me, and hold tightly to his hand.

In Possession of Fear: My Father, how patient thou art. I know thou art with me in all the darkness of my imagination and self-induced terror. Bring me out yet again, and may each onslaught be feebler than the one before, until I am fearless in thy presence. *Amen.*

WALKING

"And they heard the voice of the Lord God walking in the garden in the cool of the day." (Genesis 3:8)

I am reminded today that things are stationary while I am mobile. I move; they stand still. If I wish to see trees and buildings and streets, and exhibits in museums, and a thousand other sights, I must go to them; they cannot come to me.

Therefore, today I took a walk. I felt the desire to move about in the world. (Even when I cannot stand on my legs, my intention and the mobility of my mind keep me in practice.)

Walking is a particularly delightful occupation. This power of motion that I found as a distinction between men and things is something to be used with gratitude and pride. Visions of the generations before me who were not content to stay snug in local, fertile valleys but had to see what the wide world held spur me on to my more limited explorations.

Walking is not only a pleasure but, doctors tell me repeatedly, is one of the best means to preserve good health. And, since health is man's normal condition, walking must be a provision of the Creator for the creature's natural means of going from place to place.

Of course, the horse, train, automobile, bus,

and airplane are essential to distant travel, but local excursions are best made by walking.

Today I have varied my pace to savor the sensations of different gaits. I walked as briskly as my physical condition permitted, then I slowed to a moderate speed, and then I keyed down to a saunter. Each style has its pleasure. The hurried step causes the blood to circulate more rapidly, the moderate speed permits a thorough inspection of the neighborhood, and the deliberate loitering moves me forward but is so little demanding that I may dream dreams and formulate great schemes.

As I walked today, I thought of the verse in Genesis telling of Adam and Eve hearing God walking in the garden in the cool of the day. What a lovely picture! A beautiful, well-flowered garden in early evening when the heat has given way to shadows and a fresh breeze. All was peace and quiet except for the soft footfalls of the Lord who had come to look upon his handiwork. And he was described as walking! Adam and Eve must have walked with joy before their transgression, and now they sense that their evening stroll will be forever tainted by an estrangement between them and their divine Companion.

I find that I too walk uneasily until I have made my peace with God and can be sure that where I go he is ever by my side.

My Walk: My Father, I have read of the "Christian's walk" and I know this figure indicates my moving among men with goodness and faith and humility. May my real and symbolic walks always promote health in my soul and body. *Amen.*

SHOPPING

"I counsel thee to buy of me gold tried in the fire, that thou mayest be rich; and white raiment, that thou mayest be clothed, and that the shame of thy nakedness do not appear; and anoint thine eyes with eye-salve, that thou mayest see." (Revelation 3:18)

I have seen desirable things today, and I have bought some necessities of life. I have shopped.

Shopping is a strange word which indicates business in shops. True shopping, to most people, means comparing the merchandise in one store with that in others in order to decide where the best merchandise is available at the most reasonable cost.

Shopping is one of the things that can be done in the actual stores or by catalogs which picture the goods that are to be had on the shelves downtown or in shopping centers. The excitement of the shut-in shopper is as great as that of the one on the scene.

When I shopped I found that I was doing what my forefathers called trading. With them a jewel could be traded for food, a handcrafted chair for clothing, a piece of land for a cabin to inhabit. Today I had no gems, products of my hands, or real estate, but I was obliged to trade. I traded money which, in a real sense, represented the stored-up hours of a day that I had exchanged for currency. I speculated as I decided to trade my money for a new blanket for my bed. Was it that bright, crisp, October day that called so strongly for pleasure out-of-doors but which I spent cooped up inside to earn a few dollars that I was now giving for this covering? Or was it that hot July day when everyone I knew was on vacation while I toiled in the heat for pay? Or possibly the day after Christmas when I longed to be at home with a happy family? I thought long, before I concluded that the blanket, while not worth as much as what I was trading, was something I could not do without.

In my sadness today at the thought of how much I had to give in my shopping, I wondered what God received in exchange for the gold he gave a poor man, for the white garment he gave him because he was naked, or for the eye-salve because he was blind. And I think I know. When I trade with a fellowman I often get the worst of the bargain and go away feeling caught in a trap, but when I trade with God he is the one who gives the precious things while I have so little to offer in return. I come away with the gold of eternal life, the garment of righteousness, the sight that enables me to see beyond the things of this world. I leave behind my sins and hopelessness and misery.

When I Must Trade: Lord, I have been to the shops of the world and I have come back feeling defrauded. May I buy of thee this day and go away rejoicing. *Amen.*

ENTERTAINMENT

"I said in my heart, Go to now, I will prove thee with mirth." (Ecclesiastes 2:1)

"Now his elder son was in the field: and as he came and drew near to the house, he heard music and dancing." (Luke 15:25)

I had fun today. I was entertained.

I was taken out of myself by diversion, and when I returned to my routine life it was with cheerfulness and a refreshed spirit.

Some kind people were good enough to perform for me and others. They put such gaiety and cheerfulness into their make-believe that I was carried away for an hour or so and forgot the dour things which I had permitted to come into my life.

For a while today I had the same childish assurance of magic in the world that I had years ago when I believed in fairies and fat old Santa Claus.

And now that the show is over, I am wondering if my insistence that everything I touch must be earnest and serious is not farther from the true plan of my Heavenly Father than is the joy I have experienced just now.

Despite the tragedy and sorrow portrayed in the Bible there is a thread of joy on which is strung the lighter moments of mankind. I read that there is joy in heaven over the returned sinner.

Despite the wreck that the prodigal son had made of his life, his return to his father ended in a house filled with the noise of singing and dancing.

And the bored, world-weary writer of Ecclesiastes, who at first thought enjoyment was vanity, ended by recommending pleasure as one of the indisputably good things of life.

So when I was entertained today, I felt myself

one with all the exuberant men and women in the Bible, one with the little children of whom Jesus spoke, who piped to their companions that they might dance, one with David who danced before the Lord.

I think of entertainment as a God-given interlude between the struggles of the years. When I am pulling with all my might to accomplish the seemingly impossible task set before me and I feel the rope slacking and I am given time to rest my weary muscles, I know this has been done by entertainment.

Or, entertainment is like the warmth of a snug room after breasting a bitter wind for hours.

Of course, my entertainment today is not the main event, nor can it be at any time. However, this brief departure from the beaten path is surely within the bounds set for me by my Lord; it has been a blessed renewal of my somewhat jaded ambition and eagerness to do my best in the kingdom arena.

Being Entertained: I am grateful for dedicated performers who devote their time and talent to bringing me joy and mystery. My Father, help me to profit by the inner gift of playfulness that I find as part of my inheritance. *Amen.*

SEEING

"Better is the sight of the eyes than the wandering of the desire." (Ecclesiastes 6:9)

"But blessed are your eyes, for they see." (Matthew 13:16)

Undoubtedly I use my eyes every day, but today I am especially aware of the privilege of seeing.

There seems to be a vast difference between looking and seeing. Hundreds of times I have looked at things such as apple blossoms, pieces of statuary, country roads, and colors in the sunshine. I have passed them as though they were ordinary and expected accessories to my life.

But today I saw the beauties lying all around me, and I was amazed! Where have these wonders been hiding?

An apple blossom is unbelievably perfect and appealing. Singly it has great merit, but, when a whole tree is spangled with white, my seeing eye could well spend the day on such a feast.

That statue in the park is much more alive than I had thought. It seems so real that I can almost expect the little boy figure to rise and run off down the street.

The country road I saw from a car window was inviting and enticing! It beckoned me on over the hill and seemed a mirrored ribbon falling into the pattern of the mounds and low spots of the fields.

And what a treasure chest of gems and gold are the colors I am seeing today as the sun shines on colored windows, traffic lights, splashing fountains, and the gay garments of children.

Of course, my seeing is of greatest value as I gaze into the faces of the men and women, boys and girls who cross my path today. What goodness, what patience in suffering, what nobility I see! When I only looked at them, they were as trees walking. Now they seem to be the very sons of God.

Jesus spoke of people who had eyes but saw nothing, and he praised the disciples who used their gift to discern the deep things of the spirit.

The writer of Ecclesiastes spoke of the sight of the eyes as being much better than the wandering of desire. I think today that he meant that I might sit and desire this marvelous thing or that, that I might repine that I could not fly away to famous places and see famous sights, whereas if I only looked around me with real vision I could find equally fabulous objects and people in my own room or just beyond my door.

Today I have been seeing. Never again will casual looking satisfy me.

For Seeing Eyes: O my Father, I am sorry that so often I make such poor use of my eyes, the eyes of my body and the eyes of my soul. From this day may I be a seeing person. *Amen.*

HEARING

"They have ears, but they hear not." (Psalm 115:6)

"He that hath ears to hear, let him hear." (Matthew 11:15)

The day I learned to see with my eyes instead of covering them with a glaze of overlooking was such a wonderful day that I resolved to devote some time to testing my hearing.

And today is the day I spent hearing. When I concentrated on the amazing sounds that fill the world, I realized what I had been missing.

The bird songs that used to be an unnoticed background to living suddenly became important of themselves. Not only did they sound forth in great variety, but they expressed the moods and loves of the singers.

The voices of children as they came from school and gathered for play, which used to be no more than unwanted noise, came to my ears as expressions of joy and sheer abandon to the rhythm of physical activity.

Even the distant sound of a workman's drill, an automobile horn, a policeman's whistle, the rumble of traffic became parts of a web of tapestry of life itself.

Only today have I known how vocal the world is. From morning until night and into the night, waves and waves of sound beat upon the shores of my being. By close attention, I have been able to separate sound from sound until I have entered into the meaning of each; I know now that nothing I hear is casual. And I had thought that the world was a fairly quiet place.

The Bible speaks of people like me (or as I was until today) who have ears to hear but do not hear. And our Lord urged all with ears to use them to hear the truth.

Now that I hear, I know that God is speaking to me in so many ways, and the tragedy is that I have missed many of his messages when my ears were dull because I did not choose to listen.

Perhaps little Samuel learned this lesson in childhood from the night when God was speaking to him and he thought it was the distant voice of Eli, the priest. The older man urged Samuel to tune his ear to the voice of God that he might know his mission in the world.

Today, as I have been hearing the common and constant sounds of my formerly limited world, I feel so much richer than I was yesterday.

For the Glory of Hearing: My ears are opened, O God, because thou hast opened them. May I be attentive to thy voice as it comes in so many ways and from so many directions. *Amen.*

FEELING

"They have hands, but they handle not." (Psalm 115:7)

"Touch no unclean thing." (Isaiah 52:11)

My two days of discovering the wonders resident in seeing and hearing have encouraged me to try the sense of touch. Today I am experimenting with feeling.

145

Again, as on the days of seeing and hearing, I realize that I have been touching thousands of things daily without having any appreciation of the surfaces or materials. Today I intend to know what secrets may come to me through my finger-ends or other sensitive nerves.

I have found that there are smooth things such as worn stones, polished wood, a baby's cheek. There is a strange pleasure in stroking smooth surfaces.

And there are rough things. The bark of a tree, the fabric of a rug, frozen earth. Here again I find pleasure in exploring uneven surfaces. The roughness speaks of healthy struggle.

Also I discovered sharp things. Pins, nails, icicles, stiff grasses. Here was not so much pleasure in touching, but a good, solid sense of security. These are the warning things in life, the protective things that prevent me from coming upon something that could do me an injury, and that prevent me from injuring tender things hidden in nests.

Today continues to be a rare adventure as I touch things that are hot, cold, round, long, short. I feel the world!

I understand how concerned the psalmist was because he had discovered some who had hands but felt nothing.

Too, I remembered the warning to touch no unclean thing. Most things are touchable, but some are untouchable. Has God not built within us a great revulsion against feeling or touching garbage, slime, or filth?

The day brought me the same extension of my sense of touch that I found of my seeing and hearing. There is a feeling of the inner being, I discovered, as the feeling of the outer being. If I reach out in faith I may touch the eternal.

Again I find myself a great mystery. Everything that I am seems rooted in another existence and in another world.

Today I have developed a gift of feeling which God intended me to use regularly for pleasure and profit.

As I Learn to Feel: My Father, I know that the world touches me, and that it teaches me much when I stop long enough to see and hear and feel its throbbing. Help me to stand in awe of what abilities thou hast given me. *Amen.*

TOOLS

"They helped every one his neighbour; and every one said to his brother, Be of good courage. So the carpenter encouraged the goldsmith, and he that smootheth with the hammer him that smote the anvil, saying, It is ready for the soldering: and he fastened it with nails, that it should not be moved." (Isaiah 41:6-7)

I found that my hands could not do all that I wanted to do today, and I was puzzled. How should I overcome my limitation? But of course, there are tools for this purpose!

Around my house from childhood had been tools of several kinds: hammers, saws, chisels, pliers, screwdrivers. But I had never thought of these things as being emphases of myself.

With my fist I could not drive a nail, but with that fist weighted with a hammer I found no trouble in fastening a loose board.

With my fingernails I could not scratch deeply enough to fell a small shrub, but with a saw I could cut down a sizable tree.

With my fingers I could not tighten a screw, but with a screwdriver I was able to make a place for a picture on the wall.

The same thing happened with all my tools. My hands were weighted, sharpened, strengthened until I could do a hundred times the work I was able to do unaided.

Today, a tool to me has ceased to be a miscellaneous piece of hardware; a tool is a quiet waiting assistant to be called on when I am inadequate for the task at hand.

Tools were in the hands of the people mentioned in Isaiah who encouraged one another. The craftsman and the goldsmith, the carpenter and the blacksmith, and the tinsmith watched one another working and said, "It is good!"

With tools, the sturdy men of old shaped the stones for the Temple and made all the beautiful fittings.

As I look about me and see the buildings and pavements and vehicles, I know that thousands of tools have been employed for days and years. Men's hands have been multiplied a million times. In his good pleasure God has provided materials for tools and has given men the wisdom to fashion them according to the need.

Today, with a tool in hand, I have done a piece of work. Before I lay down my tool I look at it with the wonder that Moses must have displayed when he saw the marvel that had happened when he used the rod that he found in *his* hand.

For Tools: My Father, of myself I am enabled to do more than I have any right to expect, but I am amazed at what I can do with tools. For this extra power I thank thee. May I be a worker in thy vineyard. *Amen.*

LOVE

"Love is patient and kind; love is not jealous or boastful; it is not arrogant or rude. Love does not insist on its own way; it is not irritable or resentful; it does not rejoice at wrong, but rejoices in the right. Love bears all things, believes all things, hopes all things, endures all things. Love never ends." (I Corinthians 13:4-8 RSV)

Today I have found the Holy of Holies.

Strangely enough, I have not been peering into a place of great pretensions. I have not intruded into a private and secluded garden. And yet I have found myself in the throne room of God.

I have experienced love.

Love is altogether different from anything else that happens to me as the days pile upon days, and the years build a solid and rather frightening edifice of age around my soul. Love is unexpected; love is free; love is glad and sad; love is the ingredient that gives flavor to all that I do or hear or see. Without love, life is like a trip through a never-ending tunnel where all is dim and the

151

only lights are artificial, glaring with the intensity of a nearsighted man. With love, life is a constant excursion through sun-filled meadows.

Love came upon me in two ways today. Indeed, I found that true love is a two-sided coin of purest gold. One side is the treasure of love between or among earthbound persons, and the other side is the return of treasure toward God. When I have tried to gild the coin of love and stretch it out to one close to me, it has turned in my hand, and I and the one I have sought to bring nearer have seen the raw side of godlessness.

But love came satisfyingly and ecstatically today. I exchanged my love with another as we both exchanged our love with God. Love became a perfect circle and is, therefore, never ending. I have bound myself to one who may precede me into the promised land or may be left behind when I go out seeking the new world; but we know that our love will not perish because of a physical separation.

Today I have learned that love is not diminished by giving but only by withholding. So many need my love, and I need the love of so many. All of us grow in the love of God.

For the Greatest Gift: Of all thy names, Lord, love means most to me today. Since thou art love, and since thou hast given me love, help me return my love to thee and thy other children. *Amen.*

THREE T'S

Job said: "Unto me men gave ear, and waited, and kept silence at my counsel." (Job 29:21)

God said: "Where wast thou when I laid the foundation of the earth?" (Job 38:4)

I have had a feeling of smugness today.

I am in the family of man, and man has done such marvelous, unbelievable—yes, almost miraculous things—that I am proud to be who I am.

Just as a small representation of all that my ancestors and my uncles and my cousins, my brothers and my friends have done through the years, I can see three things in my room, my three T's.

There is the thermostat on the wall. When I feel chilly I touch a dial on this thermostat, and behold! Heat begins to come into my room to warm me. Or, if I am too hot I touch the same dial, turning it in the opposite direction, and the heat diminishes. I remember that not too many years ago men and women were dependent upon crude stoves and fireplaces.

With the temperature of my room just as I want it, I walk over to the second T, the television. I seek entertainment. I turn a knob, and immediately I am amused or instructed by the words or actions of people who do not know that I am watching them. From miles and miles away the pictures on the screen come to me in lifelike colors. Not many years ago such sights and sounds could be had only by journeying to concert halls or theaters. But now I can take my choice of what is going on in a dozen studios simply by adjusting a knob.

And when I tire of entertainment in my heat-and-humidity-controlled room, I go to the third T, the telephone. By picking up the receiver and selecting numbers on a dial, I can talk with any friend or relative or business person I choose. I have a huge book of thousands of names; I may take my choice and be in instant touch with the one that appeals to me at the time.

Do I not do well to be smug? These are only three T's taken at random from the millions of clever contrivances brought forth by my family of man. And yet—

There was another man who was a bit smug— Job. He was so sure of himself that he recited his achievements and qualities to God! And God answered by inquiring where Job was when he, God, laid the very foundation of the earth, when he stocked the earth and the seas with living things, when he hung the stars in the sky.

As this day ends, I desert my three T's and glance forth from my window and see the moon and the bright points of light in the sky; I wiggle my fingers and remember how fearfully and wonderfully I am made; I listen to the whish of the wind blowing the leaves on the trees. My three T's and all the other letters of the mechanical and electronic alphabet seem as the clumsy toys of a child. I bow and say to my Creator, "How great *thou* art; what is man that thou art mindful of him?"

Comparing God and Man: My Father, how was it that I dared to think of myself and my fellow humans as doing things that could in any way compare to thy great and marvelous works? And yet, in all humility I thank thee that we have been allowed to go a little way into thy secrets. *Amen.*

EXERCISE

"Every athlete exercises self-control in all things. They do it to receive a perishable wreath, but we an imperishable. . . . I pommel my body and subdue it." (I Corinthians 9:25, 27 RSV)

I made a doughty decision today! I am going to keep myself fit.

And this decision, of course, involves the acceptance of exercise. To be fit means to have the use of every faculty and physical power still available in my body. I have read that nonuse of muscles will cause them to shrink until they are useless forever. Exercise is use.

Another thing that I have read indicates that if I am unable to get out in the open and jog for miles over hill and dale, I can exercise by deliberately tensing and contracting muscles even while I am in bed. So I have no excuse at any time for failing to keep fit!

My study on keeping fit seems to add up to living in the way that was normal to my ancestors, whose days were filled with out-of-door labor. They did not need to watch their diet; they burned up calories in a natural and wholesome way. Because I sit so much indoors, I must eat sparingly and selectively and exercise my digestive system accordingly to my limited situation.

Whereas my grandfather may have followed a plow, I must take long walks or do an equivalent exercise to live as normally as he. My body bends, contortions of arms and legs, my push-ups and massages would have seemed a stupid waste of time to my great-grandfather. Without realizing it, he was doing these exercises while going through his day's routine.

As I have thought of fitness today, I have come to the serious conclusion that I have no choice. Since God has given me certain physical, mental, and emotional powers, and since these are all needed at the peak of their efficiency to do the work that God set for me in the world, I would be shortchanging my Lord to produce less than my quota in the kingdom. I can hold up my end only by being in the best possible condition that nature has allowed in my particular circumstances.

My example can be the apostle Paul, who said, "I pommel my body and subdue it." When my body says, "Lets' eat this rich thing or that," or "Let's not take the trouble of walking today—it is so much nicer in here watching the television," or "How about a nap instead of that muscle conditioning?" I must figuratively whack my body a resounding blow and set it in motion on a sensible diet. I must do this because, as the apostle said, I must be at least as disciplined as a worldly athlete who is willing to do the hard exercises and endure the privations just to win a temporary prize. I am working for an eternal prize of life with God.

On Keeping Active: I know from experience, O God, that thou hast given me faculties and powers for use and not for my choice of whether or not they should be kept active. May I have such an overwhelming burden of stewardship that my joy will be more in disciplining my body than in indulging it. *Amen.*